HALF-SCRAP
QUILTS

TAKE AND MAKE THEM YOURS

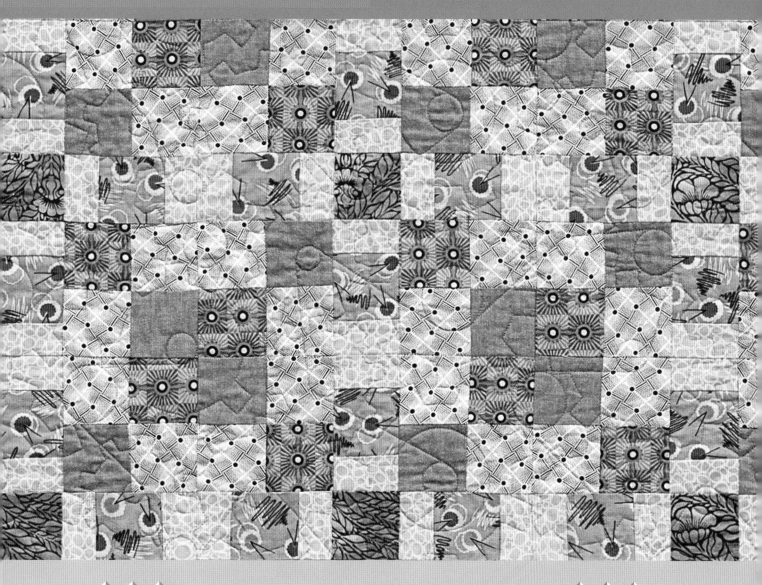

MICKEY DEPRE

American Quilter's Society
www.AmericanQuilter.com

The American Quilter's Society or AQS is dedicated to quilting excellence. AQS promotes the triumphs of today's quilter, while remaining dedicated to the quilting tradition. AQS believes in the promotion of this art and craft through AQS Publishing and AQS QuiltWeek®.

DIRECTOR OF PUBLICATIONS: KIMBERLY HOLLAND TETREV
CONTENT EDITOR: CAITLIN M. TETREV
ASSISTANT EDITOR: ADRIANA FITCH
GRAPHIC DESIGN: ELAINE WILSON
COVER DESIGN: MICHAEL BUCKINGHAM
HOW-TO PHOTOGRAPHY: MICKEY DEPRE
QUILT PHOTOGRAPHY: CHARLES R. LYNCH

Additional copies of this book may be ordered from the American Quilter's Society, PO Box 3290, Paducah, KY 42002-3290, or online at www.ShopAQS.com.

Text © 2015, Author, Mickey Depre
Artwork © 2015, American Quilter's Society

Library of Congress Cataloging-in-Publication Data

Pending

COVER: WABASH5-6830, detail, full quilt on page 52 and SIMPLY MIDWEST, detail, full quilt on page 20.

TITLE PAGE: WHISTLE STOP, detail, full quilt on page 58.

RIGHT: SPECK'S FIELD, detail, full quilt on page 68.

DEDICATION

Life has truly been a whirlwind, of late. Without the helping hands and listening ears of friends, pulling together this group of quilts would have been a far more daunting task. I won't attempt to name each person individually for fear of missing someone and causing them pain.

Some of you provided warm encouragement with kind words or by simply liking my Facebook posts. Others helped me cut fabrics for kits and generously lent me a sewing machine, so I could finish these quilts on the road. Thank you for taking my phone calls when I needed someone to gripe to or celebrate with. Thank you for genuinely being someone I can call my friend.

It has been my good fortune to have met you all.

ACKNOWLEDGMENTS

I'd like to thank the team of longarm quilters who took my tops and made them sing: Cathy Killiany, Longarm Bob of Quilters Quest, and Eddie Landreth.

Thanks to Cathy Boo for joining me on the couch for marathon binding sessions.

Special thanks to Maggie Szafranski, who helped get this ball rolling by taking on the task of pattern writing. Thank you, Maggie, for being there for me during a difficult time for you.

ABOVE AND OPPOSITE: PINEAPPLE PLAID, details, full quilt on page 44.

CONTENTS

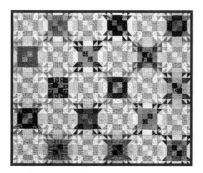

SIMPLY MIDWEST, page 20

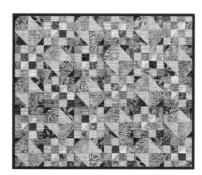

BLOOMINGTON TRAIL, page 26

WOVEN ARGYLE, page 32

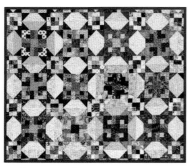

SUMMER CARNIVAL, page 38

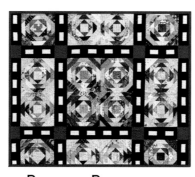

PINEAPPLE PLAID, page 44

WABASH5-6830, page 52

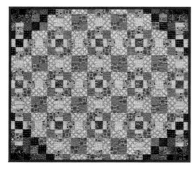

WHISTLE STOP, page 58

SPECK'S FIELD, page 68

HUGS & KISSES, page 80

OPPOSITE: SIMPLY MIDWEST, detail, full quilt on page 20.

Hello, my name is Mickey Depre. I am a quilter.

For years, I was known in the quilt world for my whimsical art quilts—full of imagery that made viewers softly chuckle. I have won awards for my art quilts, written a book about my machine appliqué technique, and traveled the country teaching art quilting.

Then *Pieced Hexies, Ring Around the Hexies,* and *Pieced Hexies Deux* were published. Someone approached me with a quizzical look and inquired, "Just what are you doing? Do you realize that you've ventured into the world of traditional quilting? Will you still be making art quilts?"

I answered, "I am following my heart and running in circles."

What they didn't know is that behind the scenes of my art quilts, I have always been a traditional quilter. In fact, if you look closely at my art quilts, you will see many indications of traditional blocks. I have always loved to piece and do needle-turn appliqué. I was the creator of the first samples for The Appliqué Society.

As I write this, I realize I have been around the quilt world for a long time. In the late 1990s, I helped support my family and my love of fiber

OPPOSITE: SUMMER CARNIVAL, detail, full quilt on page 38.

by making quilt block sets and selling them on eBay. I heard from a few of you who still have a set or two, so I know they are still out there. I loved doing this because I was able to play with a combination of prints and colors for just one set, usually 12 blocks, and then move on to my next set.

I described it as dating a set of quilt blocks, not marrying it. I would enjoy them while they were around, then package them up, send them off to someone else, and move on to a new set. I made three to four sets a week. I was a serial dater.

The traditional color combinations in my quilt block sets did well, but when I allowed myself to stray and play with combos that weren't so traditional, the feedback I received was supportive of my choices. People enjoyed how I put a wide range of fabrics together. They liked my slightly offbeat style. I was working on a traditional pieced quilt that I was convinced was going to knock the quilt world for a loop when I learned how to machine appliqué.

Before I knew it, I was knee-deep in art quilts.

After two–three years, I wandered back to traditional quilts and proceeded to make both for the last 15 years. Yes, you can do that. It's OK to do so. My personal motto has always been: "There is more than enough fabric in the stash to make both traditional and art quilts."

I was a happy camper, living a dual quilt life in my basement studio. Once in a while, the worlds would collide. I remember being stopped in the traditional aisle of a very big quilt show by a well-meaning lady who asked if I was lost. This was the period in the quilt world when you had to define yourself as a "traditional" or an "art" quilter. There was no "both" or at least not in the mainstream. Those of us who dabbled did so on our own.

Then blogging and social media became a way of life. Personally, I know when I started to blog it was natural that along with my art quilts, I shared my latest traditional quilts, too. No one challenged or questioned that. In fact, I found kinship in many who also loved both.

In the last 15 years, quilting as an industry has grown so much, with full cloth painted quilts, quilts that sparkle, dimensional quilts, and modern quilting, to name a few avenues. Today, a quilter can be both an art and traditional quilter without a sideways look.

A friend told me that, to her, my *Pieced Hexies* book introduced a very artsy way of making hexagons. That comment made my heart sing. It had been a leap-of-faith book for me, a transitional book.

For the fans of *Pieced Hexies*, don't worry, I haven't walked away. I am still dreaming up designs and pushing the concept forward. When I was asked about my next book, I took a deep breath and pitched a traditional pieced pattern book. The response was an exponentially positive one, so I got to work.

All of a sudden, I was piecing up a small scrappy storm in hotel rooms across America, as I was on the road lecturing and teaching. This is evidenced by the names and inspiration of three quilts in particular in the book: SIMPLY MIDWEST, BLOOMINGTON TRAIL, and SPECK'S FIELDS.

Each quilt pattern, in this book, is a small slice of me in fiber form. Every quilt has a story and I hope you find them as interesting as the designs themselves. I cover many genrés of fabric in making the quilts. All are from my studio, as my choice of fabrics leans to the eclectic side, with rarely a boundary on mixing prints and types. I am a scrappy traditional quilter, but maintain a few constant fabrics throughout my quilts for an aesthetic, I have termed "Half-Scrap." I hope you find a quilt or two in these pages that speaks to you. Take them and make them your own. As a designer, that makes me the happiest.

So these days I like to say, "I design traditional quilts, but I am still making the occasional art quilt in the studio." I have come full circle.

Follow your heart,

Mickey

OPPOSITE: SUMMER CARNIVAL, detail, full quilt on page 38.

HALF-SCRAP QUILTS ■ MICKEY DEPRE

Note: All yardages are based on 40" wide fabric.

The skills listed here will be referred to in every project. You might want to copy these pages and use them for handy reference as you make your quilts.

Flip & Sew

This is a handy method used for many odd shaped blocks to eliminate the need for templates. To do this, draw a diagonal line on the wrong side of a square, from one corner to the opposite corner. Place this square RST with another piece of fabric, according to the pattern. Sew on the drawn line, trim off excess leaving ¼" seam allowance, then press.

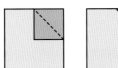

Flying Geese

A Flying Geese unit is a rectangle with a width twice its height (example: finished size 1½" high x 3" wide, 2" high x 3½" wide).

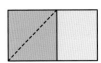

There are many ways to make this basic unit. This is the Flip & Sew method. Cut a rectangle the size of the unfinished Flying Geese unit (for example: for 1½" x 3" finished, cut a 2" x 3½" rectangle). Cut (2) squares the height of the unfinished Flying Geese unit (in this example, 2" x 2" squares). Draw a diagonal line from one corner to the opposite corner on the wrong side of each square. Place one square on one end of the rectangle, RST.

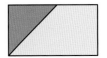

Sew on the drawn line. Trim off excess leaving ¼" seam allowance and press. Repeat with a second square on the other end of the rectangle.

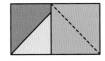

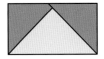

OPPOSITE: Bloomington Trail, detail, full quilt on page 26.

Foundation Piecing

Foundation Piecing is a technique used to make precisely pieced blocks. You sew on the pattern's printed lines, so if you can sew a straight line, you can foundation piece.

First, photocopy the pattern onto lightweight paper (unprinted newsprint makes a great base). Be aware that all photocopiers distort the image to some degree. To minimize this distortion, always use the same original, and make all copies at the same time if at all possible. Be sure to use the reference size box (1" square) next to each unit to check the accuracy of your copy.

This copy will now be referred to as your **foundation**.

The next step is to cut out your fabric. Make sure the piece is large enough to cover the designated section on the pattern piece plus a seam allowance of ¼".

Place your first fabric piece right side up on the one of your foundation pattern. Hold the fabric and pattern up to a light source to make sure that the fabric will cover the pattern area and extend past the line that you are going to sew. Pin in place.

Next, to make sure your second piece of fabric is large enough to cover the designated section, place it right side down on top and then fold it back over the section to be covered. Hold your fabric and foundation up to the light. Check that your patch is positioned correctly and that it will cover the pattern area, including a ¼" seam allowance. Flip back so that the fabrics are right sides together and stitch both pieces of fabric to the foundation. Stitch on the front along the pattern line, extending the stitching at least ¼" beyond the printed seam line.

With the foundation paper toward you, fold back the paper along the sewn seam, exposing the seam allowance of both fabrics. Using a ruler measure a seam allowance to ¼" and trim off the excess. Fold the foundation back into place and flip the unit so the right side of the fabric is facing you.

Open out the second fabric over the section it is to cover. Finger press along the seam. Lightly press with an iron if necessary. Repeat this process, adding fabric patches in numerical order until your unit is complete.

Make sure all areas have been covered with fabric. With the foundation side facing you, trim away excess fabric and foundation using the outside dotted line as your guide. This will leave you with a ¼" seam allowance for block assembly.

Wait to remove the paper until the blocks are sewn together. If the foundation pieced unit is on an outside edge of a section (say the edge that joins a border), keep the paper intact until the block's outer seam is stitched.

Mic's Musings

Shorten the stitch length on your machine to at least 12-14 stitches per inch. It may take longer to sew, but removing your papers later on will be much easier with the additional needle punches made by the shorter stitch.

Mic's Musings

The edges of foundation pieced units are often not on the straight of grain of the fabric and thus can stretch easily. By keeping the paper foundation in place until all stitching is complete, stretching of your unit's edge is minimalized.

Abbreviations Used

HST = half-square triangle
RST = right sides together
WOF = width of fabric

Half-Square Triangles

Traditional Method

There are probably as many ways to make a half-square triangle (HST) as there are quilters! Here are directions for the traditional method:

Cut, at least, 2 squares ⅞" larger than the finished size of the unit (*example:* If a 2" finished HST unit is desired, cut squares 2⅞"). Cut these squares on the diagonal into 4 triangles. With right sides together, sew 2 triangles together along the bias edge, (the diagonal line). Use a ¼" seam to form a square. Press the seam to one side, then cut off the dog ears (the fabric extending beyond the edge). You can save time if you place 2 squares right sides together then cut on the diagonal.

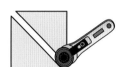

Easy Angle Ruler Method

A second way to make a HST unit is using the Easy Angle™ ruler. Start by cutting strips of fabric ½" wider than the finished size of the unit (*example:* for a 2" finished HST unit, cut 2½" strips). Lay 2 strips right sides together on your cutting mat. Trim the left end straight. Line up the bottom of the Easy Angle on the edge of the strips. Move the blunt end toward the top of the strips (so the words EASY ANGLE are parallel to the bottom of the strip and right-facing). Position the left edge of the strips even with the vertical line of the ruler where the number at the top edge of the strip corresponds with the width of your strips.

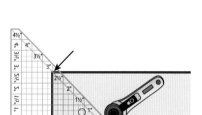

Cut along the diagonal. Flip the ruler on the diagonal so the black shaded area extends below the bottom of the strip. Line up

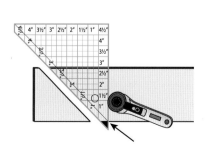

along the diagonal edge for the appropriate size and cut along the perpendicular. Flip the ruler back to the original side and continue along the strip to cut the number of triangle pairs you need.

Four-Patch

The four-patch is a basic unit in quilting. It is made of four squares, sewn together to make a larger square. You can save time by making this using strip piecing.

- Cut the strips to the desired width x WOF (*example:* for a finished 4" four patch, cut 2½" wide strips). Sew 2 strips together then press to one side.

- Subcut the newly created strip by the same measurement used to create the original strips (*example:* if the original strips were 2½" wide, subcut 2½" subunits).

- Sew 2 subcut units together, matching the center seams, which should butt together. Press seam to one side.

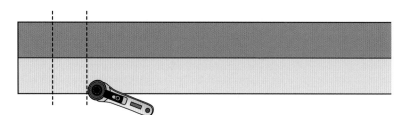

Nine-Patch

This is another basic quilt block, also perfect for strip piecing to make multiple units.

- Start by creating 2 strip sets of 2 different fabrics:

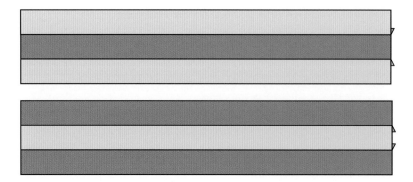

- Press strip sets consistently to fabric B or fabric A. This will allow the subunits to butt up perfectly when making the final unit.

- Subcut the strip sets into units that are the same width as the basic strip (example: if using 2½" strips, subcut into 2½" subunits).

- Take (2) light-dark-light subunits and (1) dark-light-dark subunit and stich together.

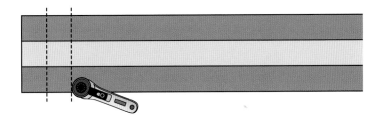

Rail Fence

This is a basic quilt block that is perfect for strip piecing. It consists of 3 strips sewn together side by side to form a rectangle.

- Create strip sets (3 strips sewn together side by side). Subcut these strip sets to the desired length.

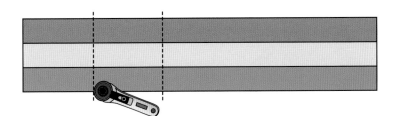 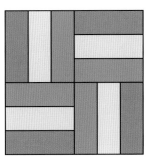

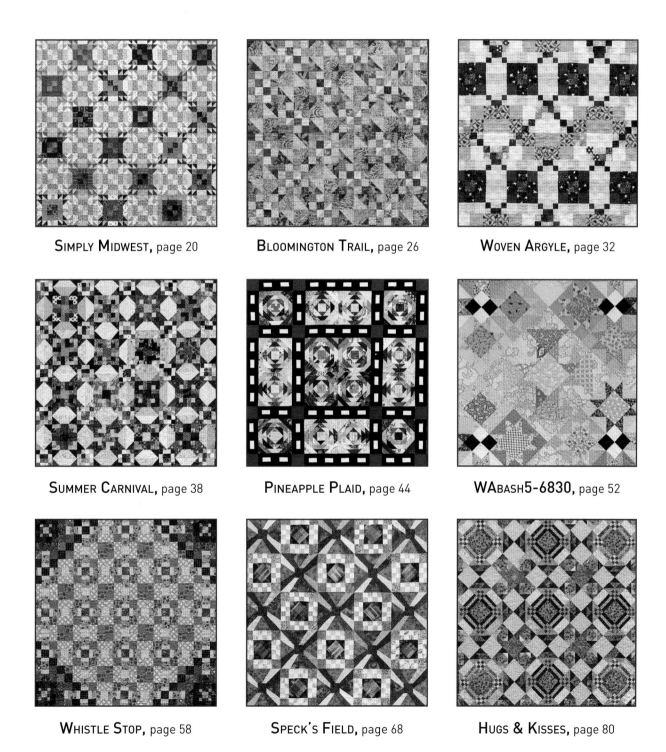

SIMPLY MIDWEST, page 20

BLOOMINGTON TRAIL, page 26

WOVEN ARGYLE, page 32

SUMMER CARNIVAL, page 38

PINEAPPLE PLAID, page 44

WABASH5-6830, page 52

WHISTLE STOP, page 58

SPECK'S FIELD, page 68

HUGS & KISSES, page 80

OPPOSITE: HUGS & KISSES, detail, full quilt on page 80.

SIMPLY MIDWEST, 72" x 90", made by the author.
Quilted by the Arkansas Man Quilter, Eddie Landreth, Benton Arkansas

The streets in most Midwest cities, towns, or villages are laid out in a grid. This is most certainly not the case in many towns on both the East and West Coasts. Most roads twist and turn. It can be tough to navigate for a newcomer. Trust me, I've been lost more times than I care to claim.

I am not making a statement about which system is best, each has its pluses and minuses.

This Midwest girl finds comfort in streets that run true north to south and east to west, and finding the center of town by simply heading toward First and Main.

That is Simply Midwest.

> **Finished Quilt Size:** 72" X 90"
> **Finished Block Size:** 9"
> **Number of Blocks:**
>   (80) Village Square Blocks
>   *(in 4 different color schemes)*
> **Difficulty:** Beginner

Fabrics Needed

Note: Yardages are based on WOF cuts.

Adjust if using fat quarters or scraps.

Note: Scrappy refers to scraps in your stash.

For 4 Village Square Block Versions:

Block A (Make 24)

A	Scrappy	¼ yard
B	Scrappy	¼ yard
C	Scrappy	⅓ yard
D	Scrappy	½ yard
E	Light background	½ yard
F	Light background	½ yard
G	Scrappy	½ yard

Block B (Make 24)

This block is not scrappy. It is made up of traditional neutral fabrics, but pay attention to values so the block design is visible. I call these ghost blocks.

Block B *(continued)*

A	Light neutral	¼ yard
B	Medium neutral	¼ yard
C	Darker neutral	½ yard
D	Light neutral	⅓ yard
E	Medium neutral	½ yard
F	Light neutral	½ yard
G	Medium neutral	⅓ yard
H	Medium neutral	¼ yard

Border Block 1 (Make 16)

A	Green print	⅛ yard
B	Gold print	⅛ yard
C	Purple print	⅓ yard

Note: This purple is also used in Border Block 2.

D	Green print	¼ yard
E	Light print	⅓ yard
F	Black print	⅓ yard
G	Light neutral	⅓ yard

(Fabric Needed continued)

(Fabric Needed continued)

Border Block 2 (Make 16)

A	Red print	⅛ yard
B	Orange print	⅛ yard
C	Black print	⅓ yard
D	Green print	¼ yard
E	Medium neutral	⅓ yard
F	Purple print	⅓ yard

Note: This purple is also used in Border Block 1.

G	White print	⅓ yard

Binding   ¾ yard
Backing   5½ yards

- - - - - - - - - - - - - - - - - - -

A Quick Look

See Basic Skills – Half-Square Triangles, pages 15–16, Four-Patch, page 16, and Rail Fence, page 17.

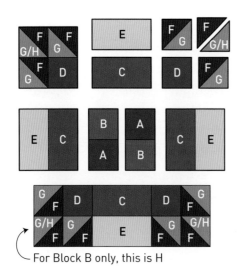

For Block B only, this is H

Village Square block assembly, make 80.

Block Cutting / Assembly

Mic's Method: Use the Easy Angle ruler to make half-square triangles.

Cut all yardage into 2" strips if you are using an Easy Angle ruler to make your HST. **If using the traditional method to make HSTs, cut your fabric strips 2⅜" wide.**

For each block you need:

- (1) four-patch unit using fabrics A and B. Cut the 2" pieced strips into 2" squares. See Basic Skills – Four-Patch, page 16.

- (4) Rail Fence units using fabrics C and E. Cut the 2" pieced strips into 3½" rectangles.

- (12) HST units using fabrics F and G. See Basic Skills – Half-Square Triangles, pages 15–16.

- (4) 2" squares using fabric D

Note: for Block B, make 8 F–G HST units, and 4 F–H HST units.

Follow the diagram to make the Village Square block.

Mic's Musings

Pick a color and piece the Village Square Block B's in pale shades of it. Try something different, like melon or salmon. You will need 7 different shades of whatever color you select.

Block A. Make 24.

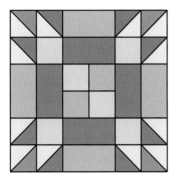

Block B. Make 24.

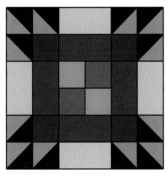

Border Block 1. Make 16.

Border Block 2. Make 16.

Mic's Musings

This one-block quilt offers so many coloration options. I keep looking at the cross that is formed by the half-square triangles in the corners of the blocks and think, what if?

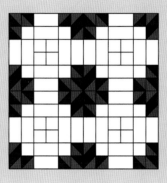

Make it your own

Play with color combinations and fabric prints. Mix it up. Break out and play.

Dig deep in your stash for some vintage florals!

Border Block 2 Border Block 1

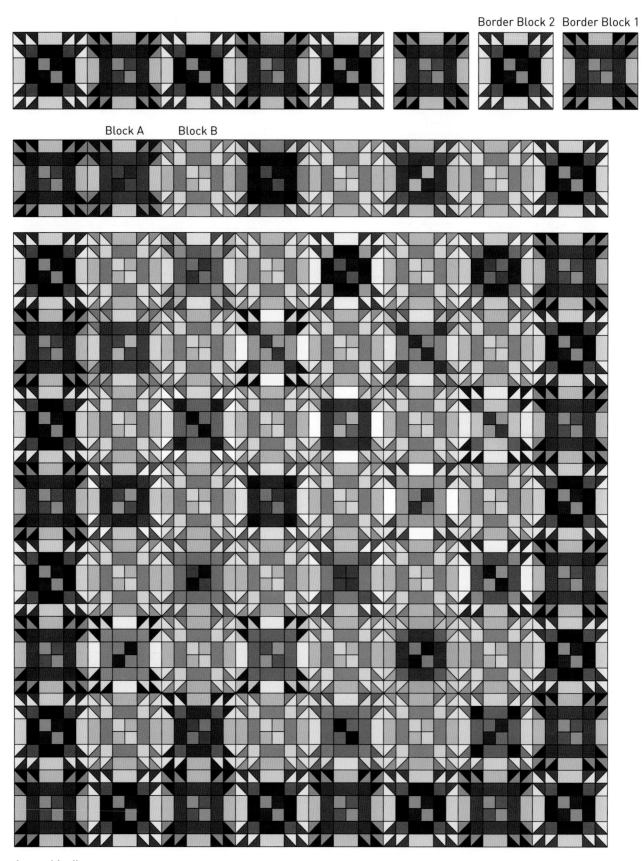

Block A   Block B

Assembly diagram

HALF-SCRAP QUILTS ■ MICKEY DEPRE

Quilt Assembly

Assemble the blocks as shown in the diagram. Stitch them together in rows.

Finishing

SIMPLY MIDWEST is custom quilted with two different feather swirl block designs in a light taupe thread. I left the quilting design choice up to Eddie, knowing his creative and capable talents would not let me down. Since the quilt itself is so simple, he flared it up with individual block motifs.

The border blocks are quilted in a feather ring design with a darker taupe thread, making them stand away from the centery. I repeated the black fabric used in the border block triangles for the binding to give this quilt a strong finish.

- - - - - - - - - - - - - - - - - -

Mic's Musings

Spend a day or two making random sets of 12 half-square triangle units to give yourself a great head start on this quilt.

RIGHT: SIMPLY MIDWEST, quilting detail, full quilt on page 20.

BLOOMINGTON TRAIL

BLOOMINGTON TRAIL, 84" x 96", made by the author.
Quilted by Longarm Bob, Quilters Quest, Woodridge, Illinois

HALF-SCRAP QUILTS ■ MICKEY DEPRE

Bloomington, Indiana—is the inspiration for this quilt. The first time I heard of Bloomington was in the 1979 movie *Breaking Away*. I think this movie was the start or the refreshing of my husband Paul's almost manic obsession with bike riding. Yes, I ride, too, but not to the level he does. I like my paths paved and with coffee stops.

Over the years, I have visited Bloomington several times to teach at the Indiana Heritage Quilt Show and at local guilds. This quilt was pieced in my hotel room during my last visit. We quilt teachers love a driving gig that puts us in the same spot for three-plus nights. A lot of hotel room sewing is accomplished.

The thing I like most is walking the Bloomington Trail. It winds through the town to fields. It is filled with people and bikes. It is the very best way to unwind and stretch after teaching all day. I also get in my steps to make my Fitbit® happy.

Since most of my visits are in March, I colored this quilt to celebrate those soon-to-be early April flowers along the trail. Bloomington is the current forerunner for our retirement relocation in a decade or so. Who knows, I may get to see all the seasons someday, while walking the trail.

(Bloomington is where I had dinner at a restaurant one night and John Mellencamp was seated just 20 feet away. I am such a überfan—as my naming of SPECK'S FIELDS and my Wild Angel Studio will attest—but those are other stories for another day.)

Finished Quilt Size: 84" X 96"
Finished Block Size: 9"
Number of Blocks:
    (72) Hourglass Blocks A
    (71) Pauli's Bowtie Blocks B
    (56) Hourglass Blocks C
Difficulty: Beginner

Fabrics Needed

Note: Yardages based on WOF cuts.
Adjust if using fat quarters or scraps.

Hourglass Block A

A	Medium green print	1 yard
B	Orange print	1 yard
C	Scrappy roses	1 yard
D	Scrappy yellows	1 yard

Pauli's Bowtie Block B

E	Purple	1⅓ yards
F	Rose	½ yard
G	White	⅓ yard
H	Scrappy yellows	⅓ yard
I	Medium green	1 yard
J	Light rose	½ yard

Hourglass Block C

K	Orange	⅔ yard
L	Blue	⅓ yard
M	Yellow	⅓ yard
N	Light orange	⅓ yard
O	Light purple	⅓ yard
P	Dark purple	⅓ yard
Q	Medium purple	⅓ yard

(Fabric Needed continued)

A Quick Look

See Basic Skills – Flip & Sew page 13 and Four-Patch, page 16.

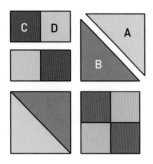

Hourglass Block A assembly, make 72.

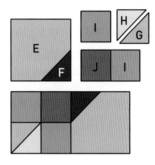

Pauli's Bowtie block assembly, make 71.

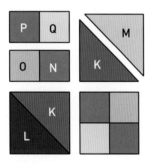

Hourglass Block C assembly, make 56

Mic's Musings

The border points fabric should be strong in color and print. Make those pieced points be seen.

(Fabric Needed continued)

Inner and Middle Borders
I   Medium green   ⅓ yard
R   Bright blue   ⅔ yard

Binding   ⅔ yard
Backing   7 yards

Block Cutting / Assembly

Hourglass Block A

■ Cut (8) 3½" x WOF strips of fabrics A and B. Using the Easy Angle ruler, cut and sew 144 HST units. **If using the traditional method to make HSTs, cut your fabric strips 3⅞" wide.**

■ Cut (15) 2" x WOF strips of fabrics C and D. Following the directions for four-patch unit, make 144.

■ Using the HST units and four-patch units, make 72 blocks.

Pauli's Bowtie Block B

■ Cut (13) 3½" x WOF strips of fabric E. Subcut into (142) 3½" squares.

■ Cut (8) 2" x WOF strips of fabric F. Subcut into (142) 2" squares. On the back of each 2" square, draw a diagonal line from one corner to the opposite corner. Place the marked 2" square onto one corner of the 3½" square with right sides together. See Basic Skills – Flip & Sew, page 13.

■ Sew on the marked line. Trim any excess fabric.

- Cut (5) 2" x WOF strips of G and H. Using the Easy Angle ruler, cut and sew (142) 2" HST units. **If you're using the traditional method to make HSTs, cut your fabric strips 2⅜" wide.**

- Cut (142) 2" squares of I. Cut (8) 2" x WOF strips of I and J. Sew (8) I–J strip sets. Subcut (142) 2" x 3½" rectangles. Using G-H HST units, I-J rectangles, and I squares, make 142 four-patch units.

- Make 71 blocks using the E-F and four-patch units.

Hourglass Block C

- Cut (6) 3½" x WOF strips of K. Cut (3) 3½" x WOF strips of L. Cut (3) 3½" x WOF strips of M. **If you're using the traditional method to make HSTs, cut your fabric strips 3⅞" wide.**

- Using the Easy Angle ruler or the traditional method, cut and sew 56 K-L HST units and 56 K-M HST units.

- Cut (6) 2" x WOF strips of fabrics N, O, P, and Q. Make 112 four-patch units using N, O, P, and Q.

- Using K-L and K-M HST units and above four-patch units, make 56 Hourglass Block C's.

- -

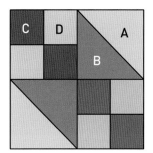

Hourglass Block A

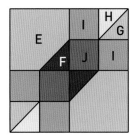

Pauli's Bowtie Block B

Pauli's Bowtie four-patch unit

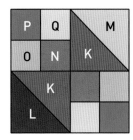

Hourglass Block C

Hourglass C four-patch unit

Make it your own

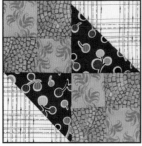

Hourglass Block.
Burnt red, avocado, and golden yellow make an interesting combination.

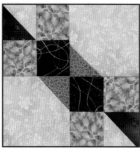

Pauli's Bowtie Block

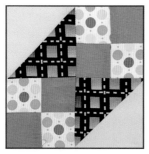

Hourglass Block.

Pauli's Bowtie Block

LEFT: BLOOMINGTON TRAIL, quilting detail, full quilt on page 26.

Quilt Assembly

Make the body of the quilt by alternating Blocks A and B. To form the inner border, measure the center of the quilt body side to side and top to bottom. Using these measurements, cut and sew from Fabric I (2) 1½" strips of the side to side measurement, and (2) 1½" strips of top to bottom measurement. Cut (4) 1½" squares of fabric R.

To form the middle border, measure the center of the quilt body with the inner border side to side and top to bottom. Using these measurements, cut and sew from fabric R (2) 2½" strips of side to side measurement, and (2) 2½" strips of top to bottom measurement. Cut (4) 2½" squares of fabric I.

Make 4 rows using 14 Block C's. Attach one row to each side of the quilt body. Then attach one row to top and bottom of quilt body.

Finishing

BLOOMINGTON TRAIL is quilted with a butter yellow thread in an edge-to-edge design of soft meandering rectangles with random small flower blooms here and there.

For the binding, use the periwinkle tone-on-tone floral print used in the inner border. I love periwinkle as a color and it is so very hard to find in fabric. I treasure it in this quilt.

Hourglass
Block C

Pauli's Bowtie
Block

Hourglass
Block C

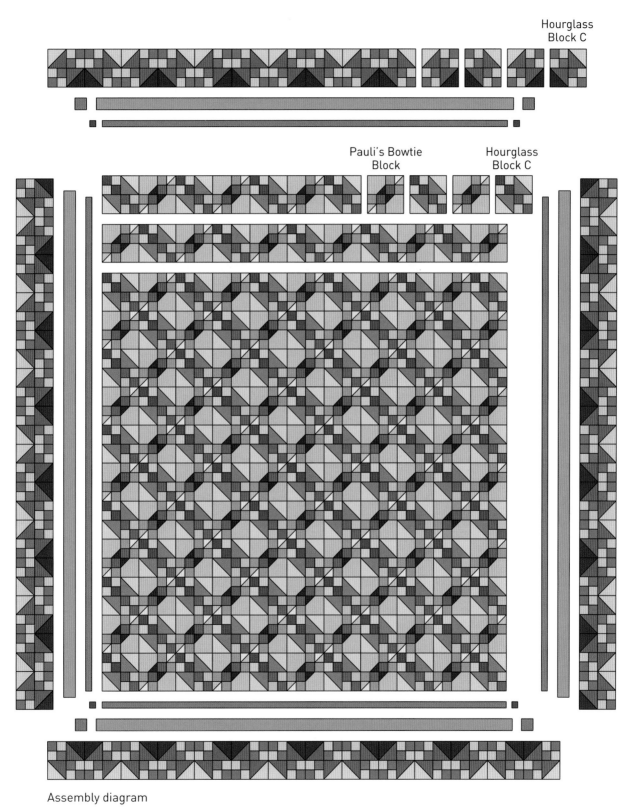

Assembly diagram

WOVEN ARGYLE

WOVEN ARGYLE, 70" x 80", made by the author.
Quilted by Longarm Bob, Quilters Quest, Woodridge, Illinois

HALF-SCRAP QUILTS ■ MICKEY DEPRE

have a special place in my heart for plaid and right next to that place, there is a spot for argyle.

To me, it is just jazzed-up plaid with diamonds. Jazzed-up anything is usually aces in my book. Diamonds in quilting mean angles and I wanted one quilt in the book to be made entirely of square units. It needed to be a pattern easy enough for a beginner, but interesting enough to entice a longtime quilter. I also wanted to make a row quilt.

After a bit of play, I came up with WOVEN ARGYLE. The diamonds may be squares, but the pattern still reads argyle to me.

The blocks of the two rows do not match up except at the block edges. This is on purpose. It provides wiggle room for beginners and makes distinctive rows that look as if they are woven together by some elaborate plan.

I wanted to play with my patriotic prints, but gave them a lot of background to keep them calm and separated. The more I look at this pattern the more I want to make a second and third. So many different combinations of colors and prints come to mind.

I hope you are as excited as I am.

Mic's Musings
Try coloring the rows in a hot/cold contrast.

Finished Quilt Size: 70" X 80"
Finished Block Size: 10"
  with a 5" pieced border
Number of Blocks:
  (24) Chain and Knot Blocks
  (18) Carrie Nation Blocks
  (4) Two by Two Block
  (26) Border Blocks A
  (26) Border Blocks B
Difficulty: Easy

Fabrics Needed

Note: Yardages are based on WOF cuts.
Adjust if using fat quarters or scraps.

Chain and Knot

A 2 different scrappy reds 1 yard
Note: For the center four-patch, use the same two reds.

B	Blue print	½ yard
C	Medium gray	½ yard
D	Cream	1 yard
E	Light gray	½ yard

Carrie Nation

A	Scrappy dark blues	½ yard
B	Scrappy yellows	½ yard
C	Light creams	½ yard
D	Patriotic print	½ yard
E	Gray	½ yard

(Fabric Needed continued)

A Quick Look

See Basic Skills – Four-Patch, page 16.

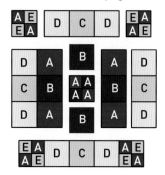

Chain and Knot Block assembly, make 24.

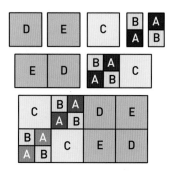

Carrie Nation Block assembly, make 18.

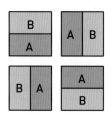

Two by Two Block assembly, make 4.

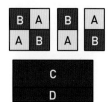

Border Block A assembly, make 26.

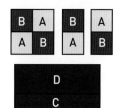

Border Block B assembly, make 26.

(Fabric Needed continued)

Two by Two

A	Gold	⅛ yard
B	Patriotic print	⅛ yard

Border Blocks A and B

A	Cream	½ yard
B	Patriotic print	½ yard
C	Red print	½ yard
D	Blue print	½ yard

Binding	¾ yard
Backing	5 yards

Block Cutting / Assembly

Chain and Knot Block

- Using the same red fabrics, make 24 four-patch units using 1½" strips. See Basic Skills – Four-Patch, page 16.

- Using scrappy red and light gray, make 96 four-patch units using 1½" strips.

- Using 2½" strips of cream and medium gray, make cream-gray-cream strip sets. Subcut into (96) 2½" x 6½" rectangles.

- Using 2½" strips of red and blue, make red-blue-red strip sets. Subcut into (96) 2½" x 6½" rectangles.

- Cut (48) 2½" squares of blue. Sew blue squares to opposite sides of the 24 red four-patch units.

- Assemble the block as illustrated.

Mic's Musings

Consider making this a two-color quilt. Make each row one shade darker in value than the previous row for an ombre look.

Carrie Nation Block

- Using fabrics A and B, sew (72) four-patch units using 1½" strips.

- Using fabrics D and E, sew (36) four-patch units, using 3" strips. Cut (72) 3" squares of fabric C.

- Follow the diagram to make the block.

  Note: Use all the fabric when making the strip sets. There will be more than one strip. After you finish sewing all strip sets together, then subcut the amount of squares needed to make each block

Two by Two Block

- Using 1¾" strips of fabrics A and B, sew strip sets. Subcut (16) 3" squares. Assemble the block as illustrated.

Border Block A

- Using 1½" strips of fabrics A and B, sew strip sets. Subcut (130) 1½" x 3" rectangles

- Using a 2" strip of fabric C and 1½" strip of fabric D, sew strip sets. Subcut (26) 3" x 5" rectangles.

- Assemble Block A as illustrated.

Border Block B

- Using 1½" strips of fabrics A and B, sew strip sets. Subcut (130) 1½" x 3" rectangles.

- Using 1½" strips of fabric C and 2" strips of fabric D, sew strip sets. Subcut (26) 3" x 5½" rectangles.

- Assemble Block B as illustrated.

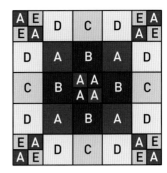

Chain and Knot Block

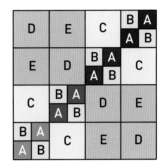

Carrie Nation Block

Two by Two Block

Border Block A

Border Block B

Make it your own

Pink and purple are fun, but toss in gray and salmon to make it a riot!

Halloween! This quilt would really show off larger-scale conversation prints.

Mic's Musings

Don't let the multi-pieced border intimidate you. Strip piecing and breaking it down into blocks (versus rows) makes it simpler than it appears.

■ Note: Checkerboard placement is different between block A and B, so the design flows about the border.

Quilt Assembly

Following the diagram, assemble the body of the quilt first then add the border.

Finishing

WOVEN ARGYLE is quilted with an edge-to-edge chain link pattern in light gray that mimics the simple but texture-rich nature of this quilt. Sometimes texture is all a quilt needs to sing.

The navy blue print used in the border blocks is repeated for the binding. Why? Because I didn't have enough of the red print left. It's the truth. I don't agonize. I get it in the "done" column and move on to the next adventure/quilt in life.

BELOW: WOVEN ARGYLE, quilting and border detail, full quilt on page 32.

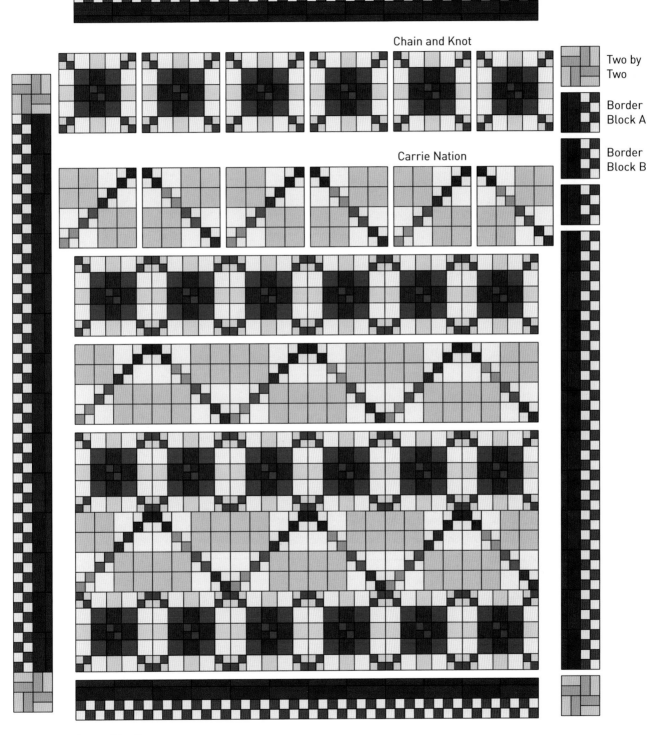

Chain and Knot

Carrie Nation

Two by Two

Border Block A

Border Block B

Assembly diagram

SUMMER CARNIVAL

SUMMER CARNIVAL, 83" x 83", made by the author.
Quilted by Longarm Bob, Quilters Quest, Woodridge, Illinois

As a child, the appearance of the trucks loaded with disassembled carnival rides was met with pleas to my parents: "Can we go?"

I'd continue to plead "Can we go?" until a day later it became, "Let's go!"

I loved the excitement of the summer carnival with games of chance, cotton candy, and fun houses. My very favorite ride was the Tilt-O-Whirl. I rode it until my allowance jar was empty (and then a few more times when my Uncle George was around). Uncle George was nothing more than a big kid. He would buy what seemed like an entire spool of tickets for our family.

Imagine my joy when my older cousin got a job running this much-loved twirling ride one summer. He would sneak me on and I would ride until I couldn't take it any longer. He'd laugh when I stumbled off completely dizzy. Just thinking about it makes me smile so wide my cheeks hurt.

To capture this memory and childhood joy, my SUMMER CARNIVAL quilt was born. A giant splash of color and chaos makes sense together for no reason other than it is fun.

I named the main block in this quilt Meems, the childhood nickname we bestowed upon my daughter. She carried on my love of the summer carnival. She'd bounce and clap whenever we went to the carnival or an amusement park.

Her ride of choice was not as daring as mine, but her glee was the same.

Arms up on the kiddie roller coaster at the age of 5, no fear, pure joy, face sticky and sweet from kettle corn and a large stuffed animal coming home with us at the end of the night.

Finished Quilt Size: 83" X 83"
Finished Block Size: 10"
Number of Blocks:
(44) Meems Blocks
(16) Border Blocks
Difficulty: Beginner

Mic's Musings

I chose to play with quilting designs in the large open fields on this quilt. I encourage you to fill those spaces with personal appliqué. Try adding some childhood summer pictures or written memories of your summers. Make this your own personal memory quilt.

Fabrics Needed

This is a scrappy quilt. Each of the Meems blocks uses the same fabrics within each block. No color guidelines are given. The colorations of each block will be different, depending on your stash and mood! *Because of the nature of this quilt, no exact yardages can be given except for a few instances.*

Meems Block

Start by making (224) 2½" unfinished four-patch units. See Basic Skills – Four-Patch, page 12. Use 1½" strips of neutral background with 1½" strips of scrappy colored fabrics.

Borders

Inner border	½ yard
Inner cornerstones	5" square
Outer border and cornerstones	2½ yards
Binding	⅝ yard
Backing	6 yards

A Quick Look

See Basic Skills – Flip and Sew, page 13 and Four-Patch, page 16.

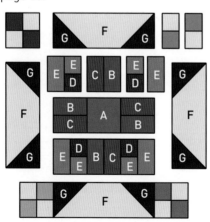

Meems Block assembly, make 44.

Border Unit, make 16.

Block Cutting / Assembly

Meems Block

- Fabric A: Cut (1) 2½" square

- Fabrics B and C: Cut (4) 1½" x 2½" rectangles. Sew long sides together to form a 2½" square.

- Fabric D: Cut (4) 1½" squares.

- Fabric E: Cut (4) 1½" squares.
  - Cut (4) 1½" x 2½" rectangles.
  - Sew D and E squares together, then sew the rectangle to the long side of an E rectangle to form a 2½" square.

- Fabric F: Cut (4) 2½" x 6½" rectangles from neutral background fabrics.

- Fabric G: Cut (8) 2½" squares. On the backside of each square, draw a diagonal line from one corner to the opposite corner.
  - Lay a G square RST on one end of a F rectangle. Sew on the drawn line, then press, and trim. Repeat on the other side of rectangle. See Basic Skills – Flip & Sew, page 13.

- Using 4 four-patch units previously made, assemble blocks as illustrated.

Mic's Musings

Since most pieces in this quilt block are 1" squares when finished, the scale of the print must be small to be seen. Contrasting color is important to make all parts of the block visible.

Border Block

■ Make (24) 2½" unfinished HST units from various neutral background fabrics and colored fabrics.

■ For each block, use 3 previously made four-patch units and 2 HST units. Assemble as illustrated.

Quilt Assembly

Sew the body of the quilt, 6 blocks per row and make 6 rows. **NOTE: Eight (8) leftover Meems blocks will be used in the outer border.**

Inner Border and Cornerstones

■ Cut (4) 2" x 60½" strips from the inner border fabric. **NOTE: I obtain this length by sewing 2" WOF cuts together. The finished width of 2" will barely show a seam line unless a small scale geometric print is used.**

■ Cut (4) 2" squares from the inner cornerstone fabric.

■ Sew an inner border strip to opposing sides of the pieced 36 block center.

■ Sew one cornerstone to each end of two of the (60) ½" strips of inner border fabric.

■ Sew each of these to the opposite sides of the quilt body.

Mic's Musings
Play with color combinations and fabric prints. Mix it up. Break out and play!

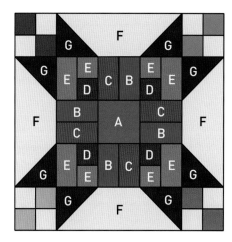

Meems Block

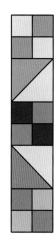

Border Unit

Make it your own

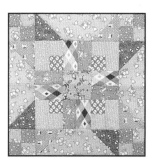

Soft and sweet '30s prints work well in this new block.

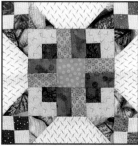

Think in different shades of the same color. It looks absolutely smashing!

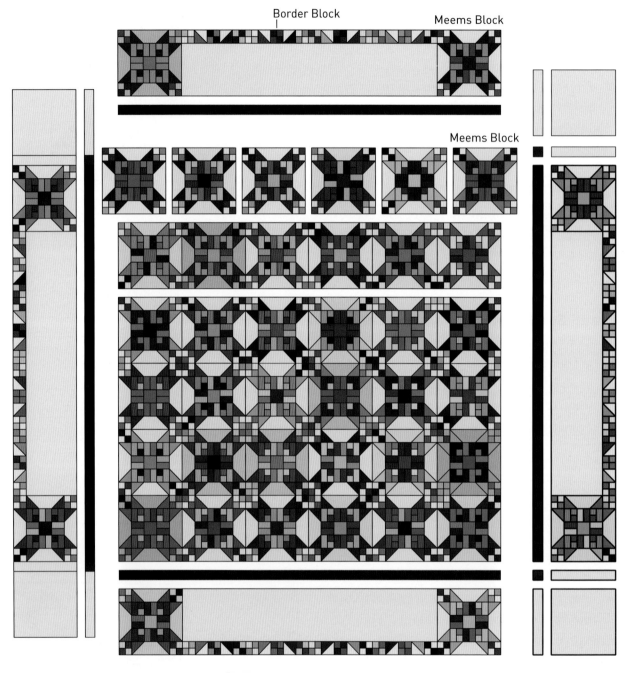

Assembly diagram

Outer Border

This border contains solid pieces of fabric, Meems blocks, and border blocks.

- Cut from the solid fabric:
    - ☐ Border Piece A: Cut (4) 8½" x 40½" strips.

    - ☐ Border Piece B: Cut (4) 10½" squares.

    - ☐ Border Piece C: Cut (8) 2" x 10½" strips.

- Sew (4) border blocks together end to end. Sew this strip to Border Piece A lengthwise. Repeat 3 times.

- Sew (1) Meems block to each end of the above assembled borders.

- Sew (1) 2" x 10½" strip of fabric to each end of the assembled borders.

- Sew an assembled border strip to the opposite sides of the quilt center.

- Sew (1) 10½" square to each end of the remaining assembled borders.

- Sew each of these to the opposite sides of the pieced center.

Finishing

SUMMER CARNIVAL is custom quilted edge to edge using a whirligig design in the center with a clear monofilament thread. This design reminds me of the Tilt-O-Whirl ride. A sunny yellow thread was used to quilt tumbling hexies in the border. A medallion in each corner gives a nod to the Ferris wheel.

Cheddar and black chicken wire print is used for binding, just for the fun of it.

RIGHT: SUMMER CARNIVAL, quilting and border detail, full quilt on page 38.

PINEAPPLE PLAID

PINEAPPLE PLAID, 90" x 90", made by the author.
Quilted by Longarm Bob, Quilters Quest, Woodridge, Illinois

PINEAPPLE PLAID

I t all began innocently enough. I was just going to make a few pineapple blocks with some string scraps and play with Gyleen Fitzgerald's Pineapple Tool. So many of my quilts begin like this—there is no end plan, just some random play with fabric and a block pattern.

I do this often in my studio. I give myself permission to play. If something comes of it, great. If not, then those play blocks find themselves on the backs of quilts. Not every quilt is designed first and then created, some create themselves as I piece.

The idea of designing the filmstrip sashing came to me when the pineapple blocks reminded me of the accordion-style cameras of yesteryear. Then I began subtlely playing in values to create the shading effect on the blocks. Voila! I was now seeing plaid.

I love plaid. It's the most misunderstood fabric in the quilt shop. Poor plaid. If you shy away from using it, you might enjoy creating your own with this quilt.

Finished Quilt Size: 90" X 90"
Finished Block Size: 8"
Number of Blocks:
    (52) Pineapple Blocks
    (40) Dark Pineapple Blocks
    (12) Light Pineapple Blocks
Difficulty: Intermediate

Fabrics Needed

Pineapple Blocks

These blocks are completely made from scraps. Separate out dark and light scraps. Plan on using about 2 yards of each value (light and dark). Good contrast will make these blocks sing!

Film Strip Sashing

Black	1½ yards
White	⅓ yard
Red	⅛ yard

Inner Border A

Orange	⅓ yard

Note: This strip will be pieced

Blue	(4) 1½ squares

Thrifty Block

A	Green	¼ yard
B	Red	¼ yard
C	Black print	1¼ yards

Note: This is the same fabric used in the 8-Grid Chain Block and border.

D	Dark blue	⅔ yard

8-Grid Chain Block

A	Yellow	⅓ yard
B	Scrappy darks	⅓ yard
C	Black print	1¼ yards
D	Scrappy lights	1¼ yards

Binding	⅔ yard
Backing	8 yards

A Quick Look

See Basic Skills – Foundation Piecing, page 14.

Short Filmstrip
Sashing assembly,
make 8.

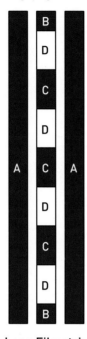

Long Filmstrip
Sashing assembly,
make 20.

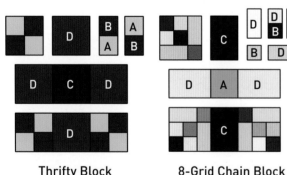

Thrifty Block
assembly, make 12.

8-Grid Chain Block
assembly, make 16.

Pineapple Block Dark,
assembly make 40.

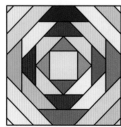

Pineapple Block Light,
assembly make 12.

Block Cutting / Assembly

Pineapple Blocks

- Make 40 copies of the pineapple foundation pattern (page 51) for dark foundation piecing and 12 copies for light foundation piecing. **Note: To print accurately, make sure your print page sizing is set to no scale.**

- Cut (52) 3½" squares of various colors for the middle of the block. Cut 1½"–1¾" strips of light and dark fabrics. Foundation piece the blocks.

- Note: Forty (40) have darks on the diagonal plane and lights on the horizontal as well as the vertical planes. Twelve (12) have lights on the diagonal plane and darks on the horizontal and the vertical planes. Trim all blocks to 8½" square.

Short Filmstrip Sashing Strips

- Cut (16) 1½" x 8½" black rectangles (block A).

- Cut (16) 1½" black squares (block B).

- Cut (8) 1½" x 2½" black rectangles (block C).

- Cut (16) 1½" x 2½" white rectangles (block D).

Mic's Musings

A foundation pattern for this block is included for your use (page 51). As I mentioned, I used Gyleen Fitzgerald's Pineapple Tool (you will want her instruction book, too, see Resources, page 93), but I wanted everyone to be able to make a pineapple block from this book.

- Assemble 8 strips in the following order: B-D-C-D-B, then sew A on either side.

Long Filmstrip Sashing Strips

- Cut (40) 1½" x 16½" black rectangles (block A).

- Cut (40) 1½" black squares (block B).

- Cut (60) 1½" x 2½" black rectangles (block C).

- Cut (80) 1½" x 2½" white rectangles (block D).

- Assemble 20 strips in the following order: B-D-C-D-C-DC-D-B, then sew A on either side.

Thrifty Block

- Cut (4) 1½" strips x WOF of fabrics A and B. Make (48) four-patch units.

- Cut (12) 2½" squares of fabric C.

- Cut (48) 2½" squares of fabric D.

- Make the block following the diagram.

8-Grid Chain Block

- Cut (16) 2" squares of fabric A.

- Cut (32) 2" x 2¾" rectangles of fabric C.

- Cut (32) 2" x 2¾" rectangles of fabric D.

- Cut (64) 1¼" squares of fabric B.

- Cut (64) 1¼" x 2" rectangles of fabrics B and D. Using these rectangles, assemble 64 four-patch units.

- Make the block following the diagram.

Pineapple Block – Dark

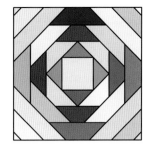
Pineapple Block – Light

Short Filmstrip Sashing Strip

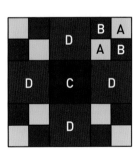
Thrifty Block

Long Filmstrip Sashing Strip

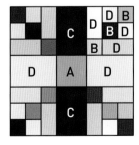
8-Grid Chain Block

A NOTE ABOUT PIECED BORDERS

I am comfortable with piecing 2 lengths of fabric to obtain the needed end length. The border finishes at 1", so any seam will relatively disappear unless the fabric choice has a distinct print (like checkerboard or stripe).

Make it your own

Play with color combinations and fabric prints. Mix it up. Break out and play.

Blue and yellow are a classic color combination.

Want to add a modern feel? Try a gradation of solids with a polka dot center.

Quilt Assembly

Assemble the body of the quilt following the assembly diagram (page 49).

Inner Border

- Cut 1½" strips of orange. Piece (4) 1½" x 76½" strips. Attach a strip to each side of the quilt center.

- Sew a 1½" square to each short edge of the 2 remaining 1½" x 76½" strips

Outer Border

- Cut (4) 6½" x 42½" strips of black print. Assemble following the diagram. Sew to the quilt as you did for the inner border.

Finishing

PINEAPPLE PLAID is densely quilted edge-to-edge using a clear monofilament thread. A simple circle and straight line design was chosen to add texture to this quilt.

This quilt currently holds the record at Quilters Quest, the shop that did the quilting, of the most stitches put into a quilt at 558,093. Yes, that is more than a half million stitches!

The same shade of solid orange as the inner border is used for binding to give a strong edge to this very busy quilt.

Mic's Musings

Individual levels of pattern visibility on neutral fabrics is much like handwriting, everyone will have a different slant. Use what you are comfortable with. It is your quilt, after all.

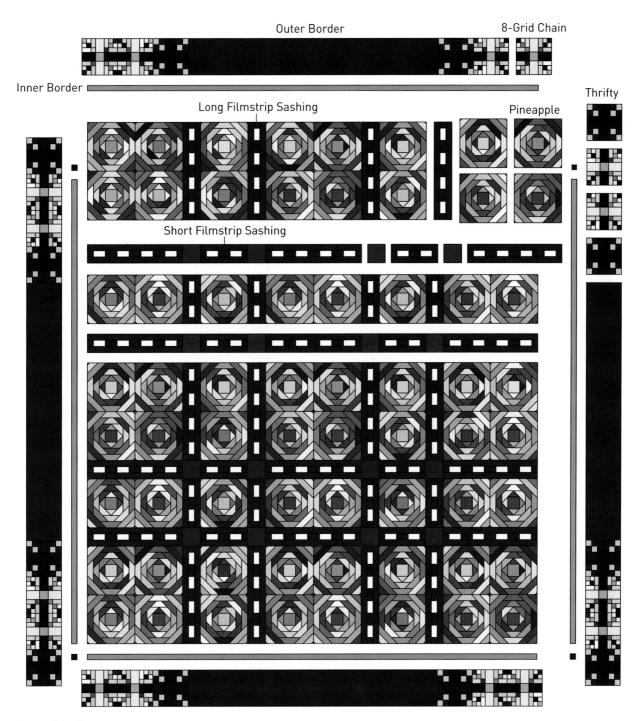

Outer Border

8-Grid Chain

Inner Border

Thrifty

Long Filmstrip Sashing

Pineapple

Short Filmstrip Sashing

Assembly diagram

PINEAPPLE PLAID, quilting and orange border detail, full quilt on page 44.

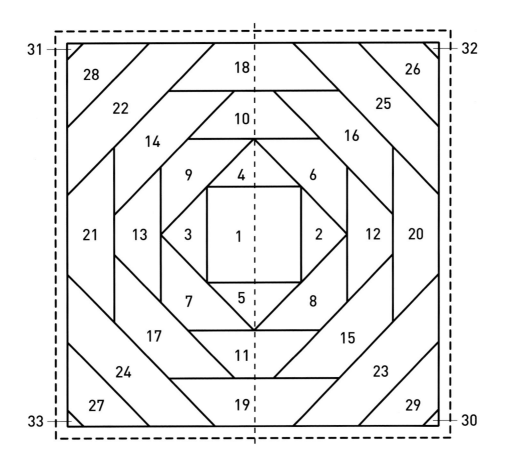

Pineapple Foundation Block
Enlarge 200%

Use the center dashed line as an alignment guide
(if you copy this into two pieces)

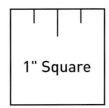

1" Square

Always check your print for the correct size.
Print at 100%.

WAbash5-6830

WAbash5-6830, 85" x 102", made by the author.
Quilted by Longarm Bob, Quilters Quest, Woodridge, Illinois

HALF-SCRAP QUILTS ■ MICKEY DEPRE

love my '30s reproduction fabrics. They tend to come to roost in my studio, and their bins are quite full. The soft colors and joyful prints call to me. This period in history marked the beginning of married life for my grandparents, Zygmund and Anna Kroll. This warms my soul. I know I had to share this love by making a '30s quilt.

However, I couldn't use just '30s reproduction fabrics. My joy is mixing them up with unusual choices and unveiling their delightful dance together. I tossed in a solid black which is not a wild stray, but is a strong choice against all the pastels. It's the Japanese print, that reminds me of a lace tablecloth, which truly sings. My challenge to you is to look beyond the obvious backgrounds in your stash and find something that calls your name. Make the background the star.

WABASH was a telephone exchange in Chicago many years ago, so the unusual name for this quilt was my grandparents' phone number. Everything about this quilt, from the '30s fabrics, to the unique combination of prints, to the size (big enough to cover both Gram and my very tall Grandfather)—conjured up memories of a quiet woman, full of joy and the ability to love big.

Mic's Musings

Mix it up! Just because a fabric line was created together doesn't mean it needs to live together in every quilt. Blend lines, colors, and textures to create a uniquely-yours quilt.

Finished Quilt Size: 85" X 102"
Finished Block Size: 12"
Number of Blocks:
   (25) Dandy Blocks
   (24) Four-Patch Variable Star
      Blocks
   (10) Border Block A
   (12) Border Block B
Difficulty: Intermediate

Fabrics Needed

Four-Patch Variable Star

A	White	¼ yard
B	Black	¼ yard
C	Scrappy warms	
	(red, orange, yellow)	1 yard
D	Scrappy warms	2¼ yards
	Scrappy cools	
	(blue, green, purple)	3 yards

Dandy Block

A	Blue print	
	(not scrappy)	⅓ yard
B	Scrappy blues	1 yard
C	Scrappy purples	1 yard
D	Neutral background	
	(not scrappy)	2½ yards

Border Blocks A and B

A	Black print	½ yard
B	Gray print	½ yard
C	Light blue/green solid	½ yard
D	Light blue/green print	½ yard

Binding ¾ yard
Backing 8 yards

See Basic Skills – Flying Geese, page 13 and Easy Angle Ruler, pages 15–16.

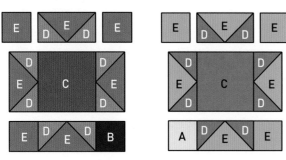

Variable Star Block assembly, make 48.

Variable Star Block assembly, make 48.

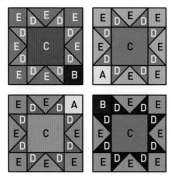

Four-Patch Variable Star Block assembly, make 24.

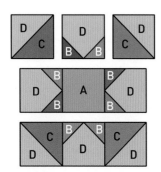

Dandy Block assembly, make 100.

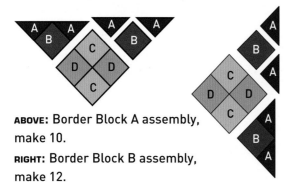

ABOVE: Border Block A assembly, make 10.

RIGHT: Border Block B assembly, make 12.

Block Cutting / Assembly

Four-Patch Variable Star

Each block is composed of (4) 6" finished Variable Stars. Keep the background and star points consistent within each Variable Star, but mix them up within the main block. The star centers can be a different fabric/color than the star points.

For each individual Variable Star

- Fabric A (1) 2" square for 48 stars

- Fabric B (1) 2" square for 48 stars

- Fabric C (1) 3½" square

- Fabric D (8) 2" squares

- Fabric E (4) 2" x 3½" rectangles

- Fabric E (3) 2" squares

- Make (4) Flying Geese units using fabric E rectangles and fabric D squares. See Basic Skills – Flying Geese, page 13.

- Assemble the individual stars as illustrated, using the fabric A square to make 48, and the fabric B square to make 48.

- Assemble 24 four-patch Variable Stars as illustrated.

Dandy Block

- Cut (7) 4½" x WOF strips of fabric C. **If you're using the traditional method to make HSTs, cut your fabric strips 4⅞" wide.**

- Cut (7) 4½" x WOF strips of fabric D. **If you're using the traditional method to make HSTs, cut your fabric strips 4⅞" wide.**

- Using 4½" strips of fabrics C and D, make 100 HST units. See Basic Skills – Easy Angle Ruler Method, pages 15–16.

- Cut (25) 4½" squares of fabric A.

- Cut (100) 4½" squares of fabric D.

- Cut (200) 2½" squares of fabric B.

- On the wrong side of the fabric B 2½" squares, draw a diagonal line from one corner to its opposite corner. Use the flip and sew method (see Basic Skills – Flip & Sew, page 13) to sew onto a 4½" square of fabric D as illustrated. Make 100 units.

- Assemble the block as illustrated.

Border Blocks A and B

- Cut (44) 3⅞" squares of fabric A. Then cut each square on the diagonal, making 88 triangles.

- Cut (44) 3½" squares of fabric B.

- Cut (4) 3½" x WOF strips of fabrics C and D. Using these strips, make (22) four-patch units.

- Following the diagrams, make 10 Border Block A and 12 Border Block B.

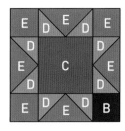
Variable Star – fabric B

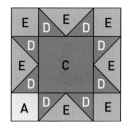
Variable Star – fabric A

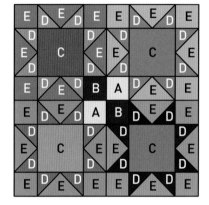
Four-Patch Variable Stars

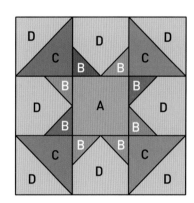
Dandy Block

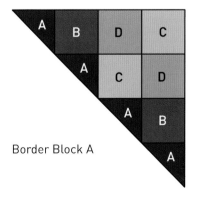
Border Block A

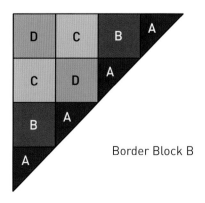
Border Block B

Make it your own

 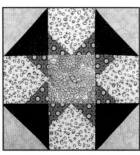

Try rotating the star centers and points fabrics around the block.

Beige is a color, try it for something more than a background.

Quilt Assembly

Following the diagram, (page 57) assemble the quilt in diagonal rows.

Finishing

WABASH5-6830 is quilted with an edge-to-edge daisy design in a soft cream color that plays to the gentle nature of this quilt. Daisies were a favorite flower of my Gram, so it just was a natural choice.

Binding with a dark blue (by '30s fabric standards) print was necessary to stand up to the black triangles that ring the quilt edge.

BELOW: WABASH5-6830, quilting and border detail, full quilt on page 52.

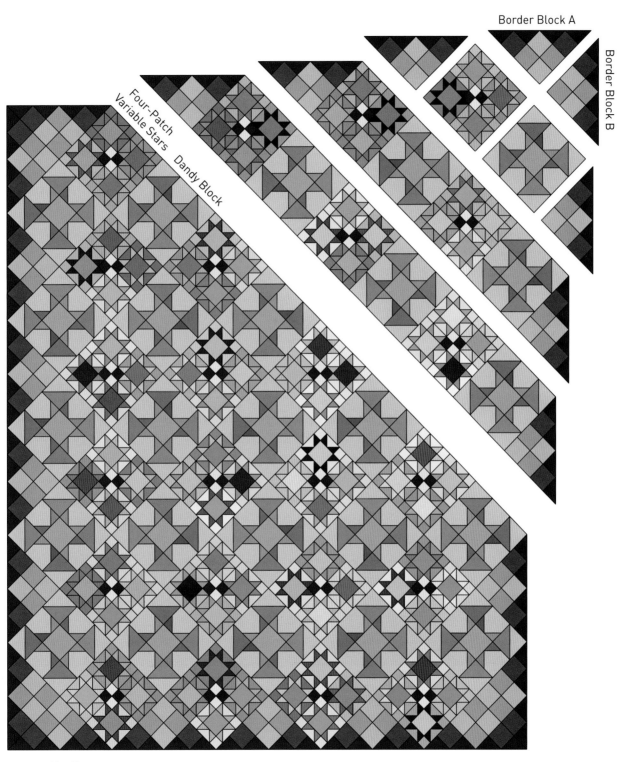

Border Block A

Border Block B

Four-Patch
Variable Stars   Dandy Block

Assembly diagram

WHISTLE STOP

WHISTLE STOP, 87" x 87", made by the author.
Quilted by Longarm Bob, Quilters Quest, Woodridge, Illinois

HALF-SCRAP QUILTS ■ MICKEY DEPRE

have known my husband, Paul Sr., since high school. We went to senior prom together and we have been a couple for a long time. He is truly my best friend and the center of my universe, along with our twins Paul and Emily.

In spring 2013, we became full-time empty nesters. The twins graduated college and landed jobs that took them to different states. After getting them settled in, we looked around and hatched a plan. The great bedroom shift was going to happen.

All three bedrooms in our house were revamped. Paul and I moved from the second largest to the largest bedroom in our 1940s home. Neither bedroom is huge compared to today's standards, but this room felt new after residing in the other bedroom for 20 years. It's that sparkly, yet nesting, feeling that you get when you rearrange the living room furniture. I love that feeling.

All Paul asked is that we make the room a bit more masculine than the previous room. My dear husband has endured 1980s mauve and blue walls (we were newlyweds we didn't care what color the room was), then the floral wallpaper with borders room, the raspberry colored room, and the denim blue and powder blue room.

This room woud be all Paul.

These walls are mocha. The decor is minimal. The colors are deep browns, plums, and grays with a splash of teal. This quilt completes the room perfectly. It is masculine, but still soft enough for me. A strong medallion-type center is created by simple color shifting of the block pieces to give the quilt a focus.

And the name? Well when one works for the railroad, anything "trainy" makes one smile.

Finished Quilt Size: 87" X 87"
Finished Block Size: 10"
Number of Blocks:
    (16) Double Patch Way
        Blocks
    (8) Offset Square Blocks B
    (4 of each) Offset Square
        Blocks C–D–E
    (8) Offset Square Blocks F
Difficulty: Intermediate

Mic's Musings
Don't look too closely at my border corners. It was a very long night when I finished this quilt, and I didn't realize that three of the four are twisted incorrectly until after the quilt was finished. Life happens and it is now just a part of the story of WHISTLE STOP.

A Quick Look

See Basic Skills – Foundation Piecing, page 14, Four-Patch, page 16, Nine Patch, page 16, and Rail Fence, page 17 (a variation of this used in the Offset Blocks), .

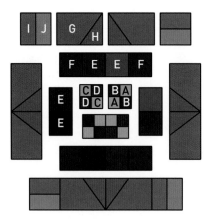

Double Patch Way Block assembly, make 16.

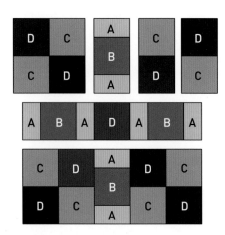

Offset Block B assembly, make 8. Follow this example for Offset Blocks C, D, E, and F.

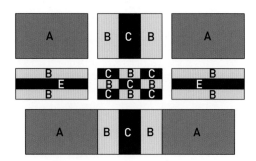

Border Block H assembly, make 12.

Fabrics Needed

Double Patch Way

Note: Yardages are based on 40" WOF.

A	Bright green	¼ yard
B	Blue green	¼ yard
C	Yellow	¼ yard
D	Medium blue	¼ yard
E	Scrappy blues	⅓ yard
F	Brown	¼ yard
G	Green	1 yard
H	Beige	1 yard
I	Light gray	¼ yard
J	Dark gray	¼ yard

Offset Square B

A	Dark yellow	1 yard
B	Dark green	1 yard
C	Medium/light blue	⅓ yard
D	Scrappy dark blues	½ yard

Offset Blocks C-D-E-F

A	Light yellow	1 yard
B	Light/medium green	1 yard
C	Medium/light blue (same as Block B)	½ yard
D	Dark blue	½ yard
E	Black print	¼ yard
F	Gray-green print	¼ yard
G	Light lavender	1 yard
H	Violet	⅓ yard
I	Purple	⅓ yard
J	Dark purple	2½" x WOF strip

(Fabric Needed continued)

Mic's Musings

Use a strong graphic print in the center to give the quilt energy.

(Fabric Needed continued)

Border Blocks H, I and J

A	Medium gray	1¼ yards
B	Light gray	¾ yard
C	Black print	¾ yard
D	White with black print	¼ yard
E	Black print	¾ yard
	Orange strip	½ yard

Note: This will be pieced.

	Purple strip	⅝ yard

Note: This will be pieced.

Binding	¾ yard
Backing	6 yards

> ### Mic's Musings
> Make sure there is enough contrast in color choices between the center medallion and the corners so they do not blend.

Block Cutting / Assembly

Double Patch Way

■ Cut 2 strips 1¼" x WOF of fabrics A and B. Make 32 four-patch units using these 2 fabrics. See Basic Skills – Four-Patch, page 16.

■ Cut 2 strips 1¼" x WOF of fabrics C and D. Make 32 four-patch units using these 2 fabrics.

■ Using A-B four-patch units and C-D four-patch units, make 16 four-patch units. Be sure fabrics A and C align.

■ Cut 2" strips of fabric E. Use a variety of scrappy blues. Strip piece two nonmatching fabric E strips together to form 3½" wide strips. Subcut these newly formed strips into (96) 2" x 3½" rectangles. Sew a rectangle to opposite sides of the A-B/C-D four-patch units.

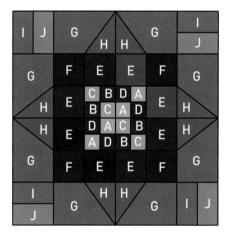

Double Patch Way Block

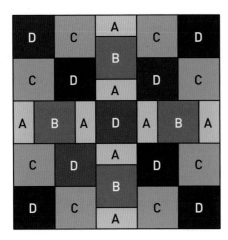

Offset Block B

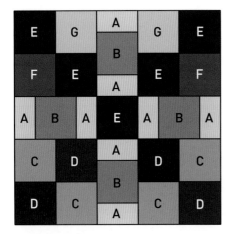

Offset Block C

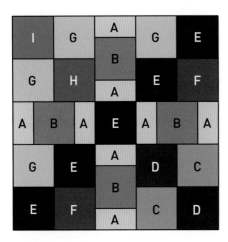

Offset Block D

■ Cut (64) 2" squares of fabric F. Sew a fabric F square to the opposite ends of the remaining fabric E rectangles. Sew the F-E-E-F strips to the top and bottom of the A-B/C-D four-patch units.

■ Cut (13) 2½" strips of fabric G. Subcut into (128) 2½" x 3¾" rectangles. Cut (10) 3" strips of fabric H. Subcut into (128) 3" squares. Using these pieces and the foundation pattern (page 58) foundation piece 64 right notch units and 64 left notch units. When pressing right notch units, press toward fabric G. When pressing left notch units, press toward fabric H. This will help when matching seams. Sew the right notch unit and the left notch unit together. Press this seam open. Make 64 units.

■ Cut (4) 1½" strips of fabrics I and J. Strip piece the strips together. Subcut into (64) 2½" squares.

■ Complete the block, making sure J-I units are turned correctly.

Offset Block B

■ Cut (4) 1½" x WOF strips of fabric A.

■ Cut (2) 2½" x WOF strips of fabric B.

■ Sew strip A to strip B. Then sew a second strip A to the opposite side of strip B. It should create an A-B-A strip. Subcut into (32) 4½" x 2½" rectangles.

■ Cut (4) 2½" x WOF strips of fabrics C and D. Make (32) four-patch units. See Basic Skills – Four-Patch, page 16.

■ Cut (8) 2½" squares of fabric D for centers.

- Using the A-B-A rectangles, the C-D four-patch units, and the fabric D 2½" squares, make 8 blocks.

Offset Blocks C, D, E, and F

- Cut (14) 1½" x WOF strips of fabric A.

- Cut (7) 2½" x WOF strips of fabric B. Following the directions from Offset Block B, make 104 A-B-A units.

- Cut (2) 2½" x WOF strips of fabrics C and D. Make 16 four-patch units using fabrics C and D strips.

- Cut (3) 2½" x WOF strips of fabric E. Subcut them into (12) 2½" squares.

- Cut (2) 2½" x WOF strips of fabric F.

- Cut (10) 2½" x WOF strips of fabric G. Make (24) four-patch units using fabrics E, F, and G. See Basic Skills – Four-Patch, page 12.

- Refer to the diagram to make 4 Block C.

- Cut (4) 2½" x WOF strips of fabric H.

- Cut (4) 2½" x WOF strips of fabric I.

- Make (60) four-patch units using fabrics G, H and I.

- Refer to the diagram to make 4 Block D.

- Refer to the diagram to make 4 Block E.

- Cut (13) 2½" squares of fabric J.

- Refer to the diagram to make 13 Block F.

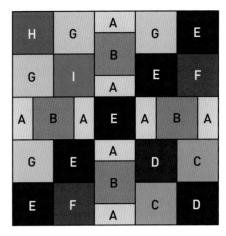

Offset Block E

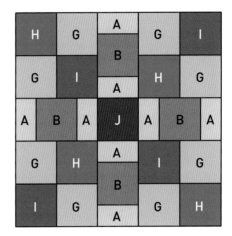

Offset Block F

Make it your own

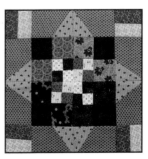

Civil War reproductions give a heartwarming feel to a quilt.

Be bold! Orange is the new black!

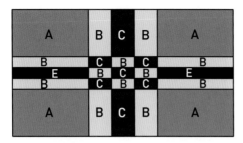

Border Block H

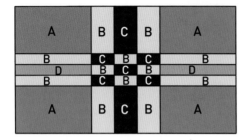

Border Block I

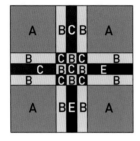

Border Block J

PIECED BORDERS

I am comfortable with piecing 2 lengths of fabric to obtain the needed end length. The border finishes at 1", so any seam will relatively disappear unless the fabric choice has a distinct print. Measure the quilt center in the opposite direction from the middle. Use this measurement to cut 2 top and bottom border strips. Sew to the top and bottom.

Border Blocks H, I, and J

- Cut (14) 2¾" x WOF strips of fabric A. Subcut strips into (112) 2¾" x 4½" rectangles and (16) 2¾" squares.

- Cut (15) 1" x WOF strips and (14) 1⅜" x WOF strips of fabric B.

- Cut (4) 1" x WOF strips and (14) 1⅜" x WOF strips of fabric C.

- Cut (4) 1" x WOF strips of fabric D.

- Cut (3) 1" x WOF strips of fabric E. See Basic Skills – Rail Fence, page 17, for these units.

- Make 24 B-E-B rail fence units from 1" strips. Finished units will be 2" x 4½".

- Make 8 B-C-B and (8) B-E-B rail fence units from 1" strips. Finished units will be 2" x 2¾".

- Make 32 B-D-B rail fence units from 1" strips. Finished units will be 2" x 4½".

- Make 56 B-C-B rail fence units from 1⅜" strips. Finished units will be 2¾" square.

- Make 28 elongated nine-patch units. (Instead of ending up with squares, you will end up with rectangles.) Sew strip sets B-C-B and C-B-C using 1⅜" strips. Subcut the strips to 1" subunits. This will form elongated nine-patch units using 2 C-B-C and 1 B-C-B units.

- Make (4) nine-patch units using B-C-B and C-B-C strip sets made with 1" strips. Subcut strip sets into 1" subunits. Stitch together the nine-patch.

- Refer to the diagram to make 12 Block H.

- For each block H, use: (1) elongated nine-patch, (2) 2" x 4½" B-E-B rail fence units, (2) 2½" square B-C-B rail fence units, and (4) 2¾" fabric A rectangles.

- Refer to the diagram to make 16 Border Block I.

- For each block I use 1 elongated nine-patch, (2) 2" x 4½" B-D-B rail fence units, (2) 2¾" square B-C-B rail fence units, and (4) 2¾" x 4½" fabric A rectangles.

- Refer to the diagram to make 4 Border Block J.

- For each block J, use (1) nine-patch, (2) 2" x 2¾" B-C-B rail fence units, (2) 2" x 2¾" B-E-B rail fence units, and (4) 2¾" squares of fabric A.

Quilt Assembly

Follow the diagram, page 66, to assemble the quilt center. Make sure the orientation of blocks D and E form the center diamond.

Border A

- Cut (8) 1½" x WOF orange strips. Join the 2 strips to make 4 longer strips. Measure the quilt center at the middle. Use this measurement to cut 2 side border strips. Sew to each side.

Border B

- Cut (8) 2" x WOF purple strips. Join 2 strips to make 4 longer strips. Repeat measuring described above to determine length of border strips.

RIGHT: WHISTLE STOP, quilting and binding detail, full quilt on page 58.

Pieced Border C

- Following the quilt layout, make the side borders using blocks H and I. Sew to the sides. Make the top and bottom borders using Blocks H, I, and J. Sew to the top and bottom.

Finishing

WHISTLE STOP is quilted using a clear monofilament thread in a gear and pulley design. The edge-to-edge pattern enhances the masculine nature of this quilt. The pattern adds interest to those who look closely and texture from a distance.

At my husband's request, I put black binding on the quilt. He was right. It is a strong, bold finish.

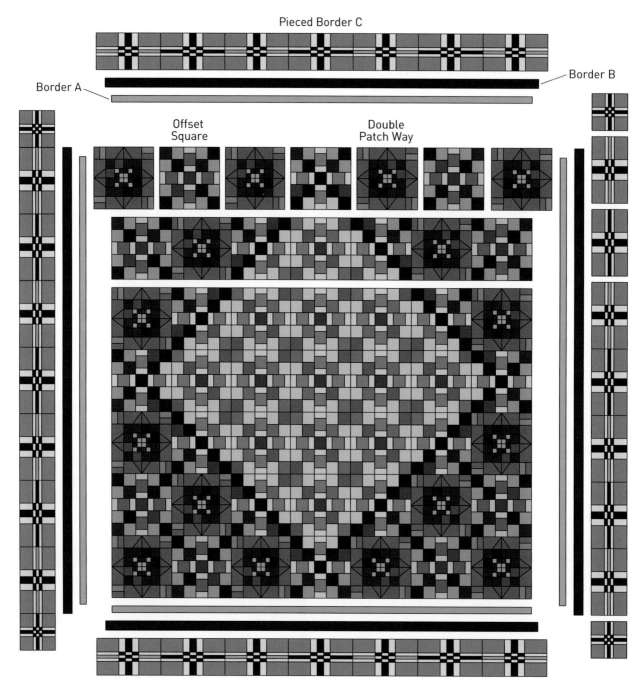

Pieced Border C

Border A

Border B

Offset Square

Double Patch Way

Assembly diagram

Double Patch Way Block Foundation
100%

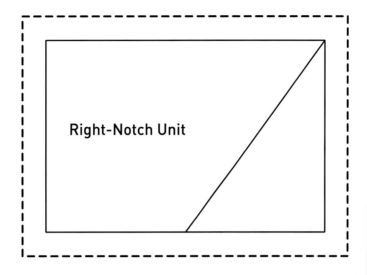

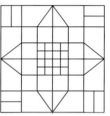

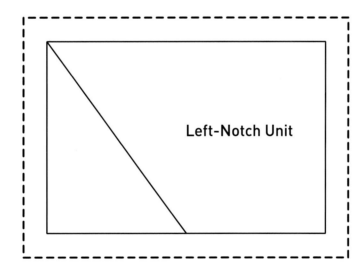

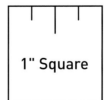

1" Square

Always check your print for the correct size.

Print at 100%.

SPECK'S FIELD

SPECK'S FIELD, 70" x 86", made by the author.
Quilted by Longarm Bob, Quilters Quest, Woodridge, Illinois

HALF-SCRAP QUILTS ■ MICKEY DEPRE

During a Jeep ride to Decatur, Illinois to spend some time in late June, with the Decatur Quilt Guild, my view was field after field of corn. This is what we do in Illinois (minus a few big cities). We grow stuff. Now, "we" doesn't include me (I am a city girl, born and bred), but I appreciate the hard work of American farmers who put fresh food on my plate.

As I sat in my hotel room that evening, I designed the Furrows Block. I just could not walk away from the inspiration that was right there in front of me. It is a bit tricky, but I have some tips for you. After one or two, I believe you will be an old pro.

I know I would be hard-pressed to survive on a farm. It's hard to find a coffee shop open at 2 a.m. in the midst of nowhere, so I will stick to creating my fields in fiber. But thanks to everyone who tosses feed to chickens every day—because of you, I enjoy eggs for breakfast.

Hug a farmer if you know one. Even if you don't, everyone can use a random hug now and then.

- - - - - - - - - - - - - - - - - - -

Finished Quilt Size: 70" X 86"
Finished Block Size: 8"
Number of Blocks: 63
  (9) Corn Crib (Variation A)
  (9) Corn Crib (Variation B)
  (14) Corn Crib (Variation C)
  (14) Field Plow
  (10) Furrows (Variation A)
  (7) Furrows (Variation B)
Difficulty: Advanced

Fabrics Needed

Note: Yardages are based on WOF. More may be needed if using scraps.

Corn Crib Blocks A and B

Note: Fabrics A and B are low-contrast fabrics. Think gray, dull, muddy, and little to no value differences.

A	Maroon	¼ yard
B	Dark red	¼ yard
C	Cream	½ yard
D	Scrappy yellows	½ yard
E	Brown (different browns used for Blocks A and B)	⅓ yard each

(Fabric Needed continued)

(Fabric Needed continued)

Corn Crib Block C

Note: Use low contrast for fabrics A and B.

A	Green	¼ yard
B	Gray/brown	⅓ yard
C	Cream	⅓ yard
D	Scrappy oranges	⅓ yard
E	Muddy brown	⅓ yard

Field Plow Block

A	Gray brown	⅓ yard
B	Cream	⅓ yard
C	Dark brown	¼ yard
D	Scrappy light blues	¼ yard
E	Scrappy medium blues	¼ yard
F	Brown	⅛ yard

Furrows Block

A	Brown	¼ yard
B	Light green	⅔ yard
C	Medium green	½ yard
D	Dark green	⅔ yard
E	Medium blue	¼ yard

Borders

Border 1, Dark red		⅓ yard
Border 2,		
	Fabric A, Yellow	¼ yard
	Fabric B, Green	⅓ yard
Border 3, Black		⅓ yard
Border 4, Purple		1 yard

Binding
⅔ yard
Backing
5½ yards

A Quick Look

See Basic Skills – Foundation Piecing, page 14 and Four-Patch, page 16.

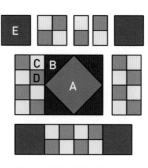

Corn Crib Block A assembly, make 9.

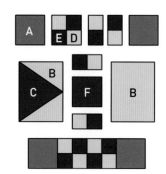

Field Plow Block assembly, make 14.

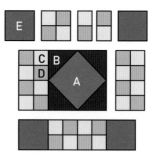

Corn Crib Block B assembly, make 9.

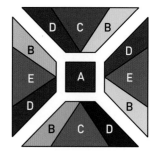

Furrows Block A assembly, make 10.

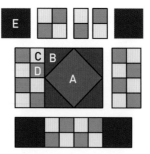

Corn Crib Block C assembly, make 9.

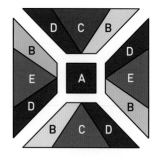

Furrows Block B assembly, make 7.

Mic's Musings

Be sure to use enough contrast in your selection of colors for the "rays" portion of the Furrows Block to highlight the dimensional aspects of it.

Block Cutting / Assembly

Corn Crib Blocks A and B

- Make 32 copies of Square in a Square (SnS) (page 78) foundation paper piecing pattern. **Note: To print accurately, make sure your print page sizing is set No Scale.**

- Fabric A, cut (18) 3½" squares.

- Fabric B, cut (36) 3" squares, then cut each square in half on the diagonal.

- Foundation paper piece (18) SnS using fabrics A and B.

- Fabric C, cut (18) 1½" x 25" strips.

- Fabric D, cut 1½" x 25" strips of each yellow to be used. Use yellows consistently within a block, but scrappy throughout the quilt.

- Make 144 four-patch units using fabrics C and D, along with another 8 for each block.

- Fabric E, cut (36) 2½" squares of each brown.

- Make 9 Corn Crib 1 and (9) Corn Crib 2 blocks. **Note: Always keep the checkerboard arrangement of the four-patch units consistent in all the blocks to allow the design to show.**

Corn Crib Block C

- Fabric A, cut (14) 3½" squares.

- Fabric B, cut (28) 3½" squares. Cut each square in half on the diagonal.

- Foundation paper piece (14) SnS using fabrics A and B.

- Fabric C, cut (14) 1½" x 25" strips.

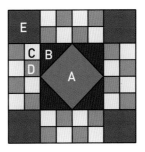

Corn Crib Block A

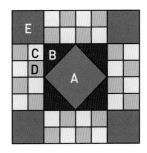

Corn Crib Block B

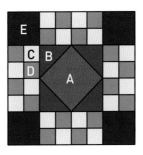

Corn Crib Block C

Fabric D, cut (14) 1½" x 25" strips of each orange fabric. Use the oranges consistently within a block, but keep them scrappy throughout the quilt.

Make (112) four-patch units using fabrics C and D, along with another 8 for each block.

Fabric E, cut (56) 3½" squares.

Make (14) Corn Crib 3. **Note: Always keep checkerboard arrangement of four-patch units consistent in all blocks to allow the design to play out.**

I used the Tri Tool ruler from this set.

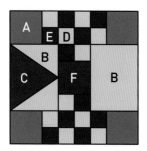

Field Plow Block

Field Plow Block

Fabric A, cut (56) 2½" squares.

Fabric B, cut (14) 3½" x 4½" rectangles. Cut (28) 2½" X 4½" rectangles.

Fabric C, cut (14) 4" x 5" rectangles.

Foundation paper piece (14) Field Plow (page 78) blocks using fabrics C and B. Make them into 2½" x 4½" rectangles. (For foundation see page 78.)

Fabric D, cut (14) 1½" x 16" strips of each light blue.

Fabric E, cut (14) 1½" x 16" strips of each medium blue. Blues are used consistently within each block but are scrappy throughout the quilt.

Mic's Musings

While this quilt was inspired by the cornfields of Illinois, the design lends itself nicely to show off many combinations of fabric.

- Fabric F, cut (14) 2½" squares.

- Sew strip sets of fabrics D and E. Cut each strip set into (10) 1½" x 2½" rectangles. Form (4) four-patch units from (8) rectangles. Sew the remaining (2) rectangles onto opposite sides of (1) fabric F square.

- Assemble (14) blocks as illustrated. **Note: Keep the four-patch orientation consistent to create an overall pattern.**

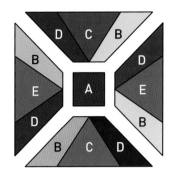

Furrows Block A

Furrows Block

- Make 68 copies of the Furrows foundation paper (page 79).

- Fabric A, cut (17) 2½" squares.

- Fabric B, cut (68) 2½" x 5½" rectangles.

- Fabric C, cut 4" strips of fabric. Using a 60 degree ruler at the 4½" line, cut 44 triangles.

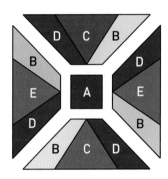

Furrows Block B

- Fabric D, cut (68) 2½" x 5½" rectangles.

- Fabric E, cut 4" strips of the fabric. Using a 60 degree ruler at the 4½" line, cut (24) triangles.

- Foundation paper piece 44 units using fabrics B, C and D.

- Foundation paper piece 24 units using fabrics B, E and D.

- Trim the units.

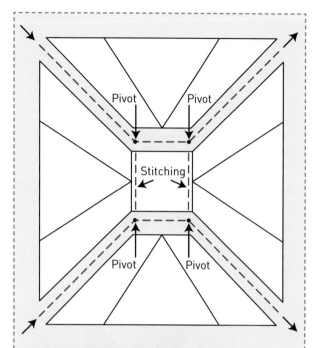

Furrows Sewing Guide

Stitch one unit to a side, starting at one outer edge until the inner corner edge seam allowance is reached. Pivot then sew across the top of the unit to square it until the inner corner edge seam allowance is reached. Pivot again then sew the opposite outer edge to the end. Repeat on the opposite side. Press block and trim as needed.

FURROWS BLOCK TIP

Sew one foundation unit to the center square. *Never* sew into the seam allowance. Do the same for the opposite side. Proceed to sew each of the remaining units using the Y seam method when you reach the center square. Remember, *Never* sew into the seam allowance.

- Assemble 10 blocks using 3 B-C-D units and 1 B-E-D unit.

- Assemble 7 blocks using 2 B-C-D units and 2 B-E-D units.

- Stitch one unit to 2½" square, starting and stopping ½" from each edge. Repeat on the opposite side.

Pieced Border 2

- Fabric A, cut (5) 2½" x WOF strips. Cut (4) 2½" x 8½" rectangles then cut (4) 2½" squares. **If you're using the traditional method to make HSTs, cut 4 of the fabric strips 2⅞" wide.**

- Fabric B, cut 2½" x WOF strips. (The number will depend on the size of the scraps used.) **If you're using the traditional method to make HSTs, cut your fabric strips 2⅞" wide**

- Border 1 fabric, cut (8) 1½" x 2½" rectangles.

- Using 2½" strips of fabrics A and B along with the Easy Angle ruler, cut (112) units. See Basic Skills – Half-Square Triangles, pages 15-16.

- Assemble 2 side borders by piecing 1 border 1 rectangle, 16 HST units, (1) 2½" x 8½" rectangle of fabric A, 16 HST units and 1 border 1 rectangle. See the assembly diagram for the proper orientation of the HST units.

- For the top border assemble it in the following order: (1) 2½" square of fabric A, 1 border 1 rectangle, 12 HST units, (1) 2½" x 8½" rectangle of fabric A. Assemble the bottom border in the following order: 12 HST units, 1 border 1 rectangle and (1) 2½" square of fabric A.

Quilt Assembly

Assemble the body of the quilt using the assembly diagram (page 76).

Border 1

■ Stitch together (2) 1½" x 56½" strips and (2) 1½" x 72½" strips. Cut (4) 1½" squares of Border 3 fabric. Sew one square on each end of the shorter strips. Sew longer strips on each side. Sew the 2 remaining strips on the top and bottom.

Border 2

■ Attach Border 2 by applying the 2 side borders first, then top and bottom.

Border 3

■ Stitch together (2) 1½" x 64½" strips and (2) 1½" x 78½" strips. Sew the longer strips on each side. Sew the shorter strips on the top and bottom.

Border 4

■ Stitch together (2) 3½" x 70½" strips and (2) 3½" x 80½" strips. Sew the longer strips on each side. Sew the shorter strips on the top and bottom.

Make it your own

Try using several shades of red then toss in black and aqua for a zippy colorway.

Scrappy and '30s prints also work well with the small pieces of this block.

Make an English Garden version of this quilt using florals.

Border 4

Border 3

Border 2

Border 1

Field Plow
Block

Corn Crib
Block C

Corn Crib
Block A

Furrows
Block

Corn Crib
Block B

Assembly diagram

Finishing

SPECK'S FIELD is quilted with an avocado green thread in an edge-to-edge pattern that mimics the look of the cross-hatching pattern farmers use to sow their fields. This pattern is evident from my airplane seat window and always welcomes me back to my Midwest home when I travel. Binding is a continuation of the solid looking blue fabric in the border for a soft, blended edge.

BELOW: SPECK'S FIELD, quilting detail, full quilt on page 68.

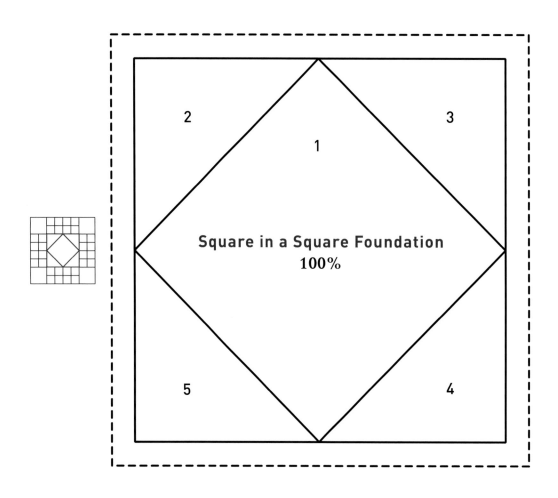

2   3

1

Square in a Square Foundation
100%

5   4

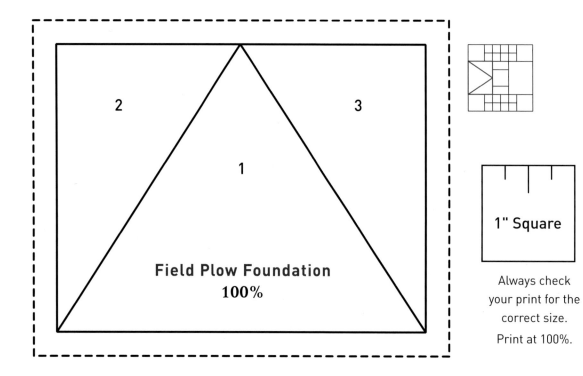

2   3

1

Field Plow Foundation
100%

1" Square

Always check
your print for the
correct size.
Print at 100%.

Furrows Block Foundation
100%

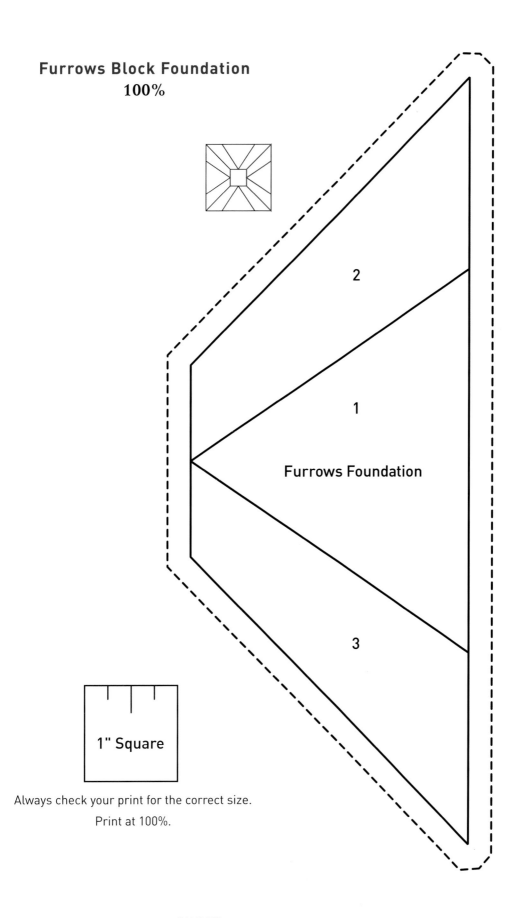

Furrows Foundation

2

1

3

1" Square

Always check your print for the correct size.

Print at 100%.

Hugs & Kisses

Hugs & Kisses, 70" x 86", made by the author.
Quilted by Cathy Killiany, Massillon, Ohio

We all have conversation prints that we tend to collect. These would be the prints that catch your eye or that you connect with personally. Love coffee? There is a print for you. You're a nurse? There are prints for that, too. Share your home with a dachshund? Yes, there's a print!

My weakness is cherry prints. I love cherries. My cherry print stash is quite large. In my lifetime, there will be several cherry quilts completed and still more quilt tops to leave in the Will.

I got excited a few years back when I stumbled onto three fat quarters of a cherry print I had never encountered before. It was an odd retro print reminiscent of the '40s. It was a beautiful showstopper with its muted palette and all three fat quarters were added to my stash.

When it came time to start designing for this book, I knew those cherries were going to be in the very first quilt I designed. They were also going to be the only conversation print in the quilt. With only ¾ yard on hand, I had to use them sparingly, but that was a good thing. Conversation prints seem to sing louder when they are alone in a quilt or have minimal backup.

The yardage indicated for the focus fabric is 1 yard. I used those three fat quarters and there was not even an inch strip of fabric left when I was done. I am giving you some wiggle room. Things happen and the rotary cutter has a mind of its own sometimes.

There are a lot of pieces to this quilt. It's not for the faint of heart. If you love something, you want to smother it with hugs and kisses and let it shine in a semi-scrappy quilt like this.

Check your stash. I am betting you have a yard of a much-loved conversation print to get started with right now.

Finished Quilt Size: 85" X 85"
Finished Block Size: 12"
Number of Blocks: 63
    (25) Missouri Puzzle Blocks
       with 3 color Variations
    (16) Santa Fe Trail Blocks
Difficulty: Advanced

Fabrics Needed

Note: Yardages are based on WOF cuts. Adjust if using fat quarters or scraps.

Note: The ¹³⁄₁₆" mark is located between the ¾" and ⅞" on the ruler.

Missouri PuzzleBlock, Santa Fe Trail Block, and Border Units

A	Focus fabric	1 yard
B	Assorted creams/taupes	
		2 yards

Missouri Puzzle Blocks (A, B, C)

C	Assorted deep reds	1 yard
D	Dark blue (#1)	1 yard
E	Gray/blue	¾ yard
F	Light/medium blue	1 yard
G	Pink/red	½ yard

Missouri Puzzle Block A

H	Dark blue (#2)	¼ yard
I	Lime green	¼ yard

Missouri Puzzle Block B

J	Dark green	⅓ yard
K	Medium green	¼ yard

Missouri Puzzle Block C

L	Dark blue (#3)	¼ yard
M	Avocado green	⅓ yard

Santa Fe Trail Block

N	Scrappy greens	⅔ yard
O	Scrappy blues	1⅓ yards
P	Pink	¼ yard
Q	Medium blue	¼ yard

Border and Corner Units

R	Red	½ yard
S	Green	½ yard
T	Light green	½ yard
U	Dark green	½ yard
V	Light raspberry	½ yard
W	Dark raspberry	½ yard

Binding	⅔ yard
Backing	6 yards

IMPORTANT – READ THIS!

Accuracy in cutting and stitching is extremely important for both the Missouri Puzzle and the Santa Fe Trail blocks. Before cutting all your units, cut and sew each of the nine-patch units and the rail fence unit. Make any adjustments needed to your seam allowances before proceeding with the rest of the blocks. For the Missouri Puzzle Block, the unfinished nine-patch units should measure 2½" square and the unfinished rail fence units should measure 2½" x 4½". For the Santa Fe Trail block, the unfinished nine-patch units should measure 4½" square. Although it is tempting to sew long strip sets, in this case it will be more accurate to cut the individual pieces.

A Quick Look

See Basic Skills – Foundation Piecing, page 14, Half-Square Triangle, pages 15–16, and Four-Patch, page 16.

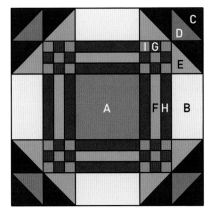

Missouri Puzzle Block A, make 5.

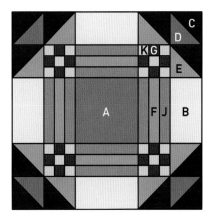

Missouri Puzzle Block B, make 8.

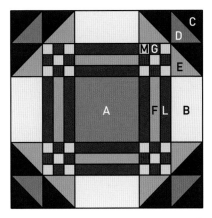

Missouri Puzzle Block C, make 12.

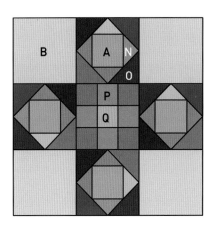

Santa Fe Trail assembly, make 16.

Mic's Musings

Use a small scale striped fabric in the Missouri Puzzle block for a dynamic look.

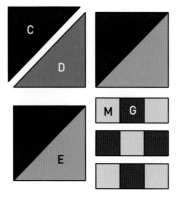

Missouri Puzzle Block all variations corner unit sassembly

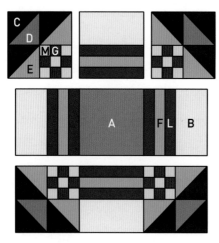

Missouri Puzzle Block all variations

Block Cutting

Missouri Puzzle Block, All Variations

- Fabric A: (25) 4½" squares

- Fabric B: (100) 2½" x 4½" rectangles

- Fabric C: (150) 2⅞" squares cut on the diagonal to make 300 triangles. See Basic Skills – Half-Square Triangles (using the traditional method), page 15.

- Fabric D: (50) 2⅞" squares cut on the diagonal to make 100 triangles

- Fabric E: (100) 2⅞" squares cut on the diagonal to make 200 triangles

- Fabric F: (100) 1³⁄₁₆" x 4½" rectangles.
  Note: ³⁄₁₆" is inbetween the ⅛" and ¼" mark.

- Fabric G: (400) 1³⁄₁₆" squares

Missouri Puzzle Block A

- Fabric H: (40) 1³⁄₁₆" x 4½" rectangles.
  Note: ¹³⁄₁₆" mark is inbetween the ¾" and ⅞" mark.

- Fabric I: (100) 1³⁄₁₆" squares

Missouri Puzzle Block B

- Fabric J: (64) 1³⁄₁₆" x 4½" rectangles

- Fabric K: (160) 1³⁄₁₆" squares

Missouri Puzzle Block C

- Fabric L: (96) 1³⁄₁₆" x 4½" rectangles

- Fabric M: (240) 1³⁄₁₆" squares

Santa Fe Trail Block

- Fabric N: (64) 3½" squares cut on the diagonal twice to make 256 triangles

- Fabric O: (128) 3¼" squares cut on the diagonal once to make 256 triangles

- Fabric P: (64) 1³⁄₁₆" squares.
  Note: ¹³⁄₁₆th is in between the ¾ and ⁷⁄₈ mark.

- Fabric Q: (80) 1³⁄₁₆" squares

- Fabric A: (64) 2½" squares

- Fabric B: (64) 4½" squares

Borders and Corner Units

- Fabric D: (64) 2½" squares

- Fabric B: (64) 2½" squares

- Fabric R: (18) 4⅞" squares cut on the diagonal once

- Fabric S: (18) 4⅞" squares cut on the diagonal once. See Basic Skills – Half Square Triangles, pages 15–16.

- Fabric T: (28) 2¾" squares

- Fabric U: (28) 2¾" squares

- Fabric V: (54) 3¼" squares cut on the diagonal once to make 108 triangles

- Fabric W: (54) 3¼" squares cut on the diagonal once to make 108 triangles

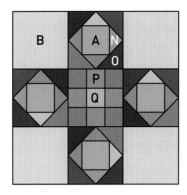

Santa Fe Trail Block, make 16.

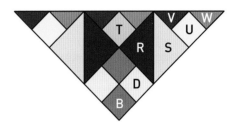

Border Unit 1, make 8.

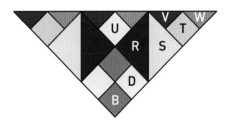

Border Unit 2, make 8.

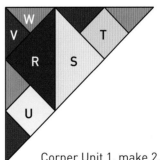

Corner Unit 1, make 2.

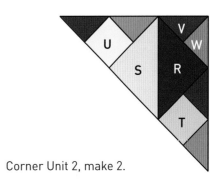

Corner Unit 2, make 2.

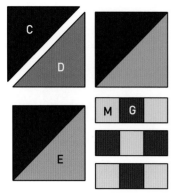

Missouri Puzzle Block corner unit assembly

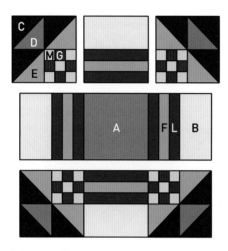

Missouri Puzzle Block assembly

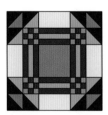

Block A

Block B

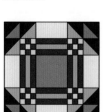

Block C

Block Assembly

The Missouri Puzzle block has three separate color schemes, but the directions for assembling the blocks are all the same. Although this looks complicated, it is just a nine-patch block. The corner units are each a four-patch.

Missouri Puzzle Blocks

- Sew 100 HST using fabrics C and D.

- Sew 200 HST using fabrics C and E.

Missouri Puzzle Block A

- Sew 20 nine-patch units using fabrics G and I.

- Sew 20 rail fence units using fabrics F and H.

Missouri Puzzle Block B

- Sew 32 nine-patch units using fabrics G and K.

- Sew 32 rail fence units using fabrics F and J.

Missouri Puzzle Block C

- Sew 48 nine-patch units using fabrics G and M.

- Sew 48 rail fence units using fabrics F and L.

■ Referring to the diagram, assemble the corner units. Make sure the fabric C pieces are all facing the same direction. Each corner unit should measure 4½" square unfinished.

■ Sew the rail fence units to fabric B (2½" x 4½") rectangles. These units should measure 4½" square unfinished.

■ Assemble the entire block as a nine patch.

Santa Fe Trail Block

■ Sew (16) nine-patch units using fabrics P and Q.

■ The square-in-a-square-in-a-square block is foundation paper pieced. Make 64 copies of the foundation pattern (page 91). **Note: To print accurately, make sure your print page sizing is set No Scale.** Check to make sure your copy of the printed pattern is 4" finished. Make adjustments as needed for accuracy.

■ Foundation paper piece the block using fabric A in the center, fabric N for the inner square, and fabric O for the outer square.

■ Referring to the diagram, assemble the entire block as a nine patch, using fabric B 4½" squares in the corners, the nine-patch in the center, and the square-in-a-square-in-a-square units on the sides.

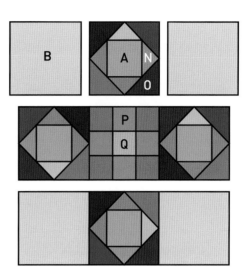

Santa Fe Trail Block assembly

Mic's Musings

Consider scrapping up this quilt even more by using the same print in three different colorways for the center squares of the Santa Fe Trail Block.

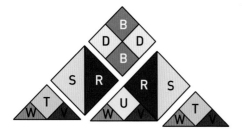

Assemble 4 Border Version A triangles

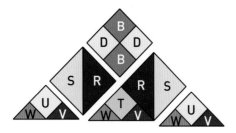

Assemble 4 Border Version B triangles

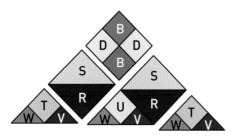

Assemble 4 Border Version C triangles

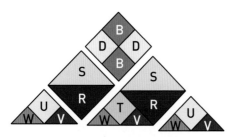

Assemble 4 Border Version D triangles

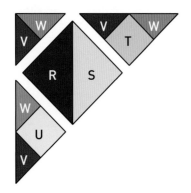

Assemble 2 corner Version A triangles

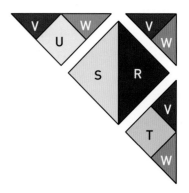

Assemble 2 corner Version B triangles

Border Triangles and Corner Triangles

■ There are four versions of the border triangles and the corner triangles. This is done so that the medium and dark green squares alternate.

■ Sew 32 HST units using fabrics R and S.

■ Sew 16 four-patch units using fabrics B and D.

■ Foundation paper piece 56 border triangle units, to make 28 blocks using fabrics T, V, and W. Make an additional 28 using fabrics U, V, and W. Assemble the 4 Border Version A triangles.

Quilt Assembly

Following the assembly diagram. Arrange the blocks. Sew the blocks into diagonal rows, then sew the rows together.

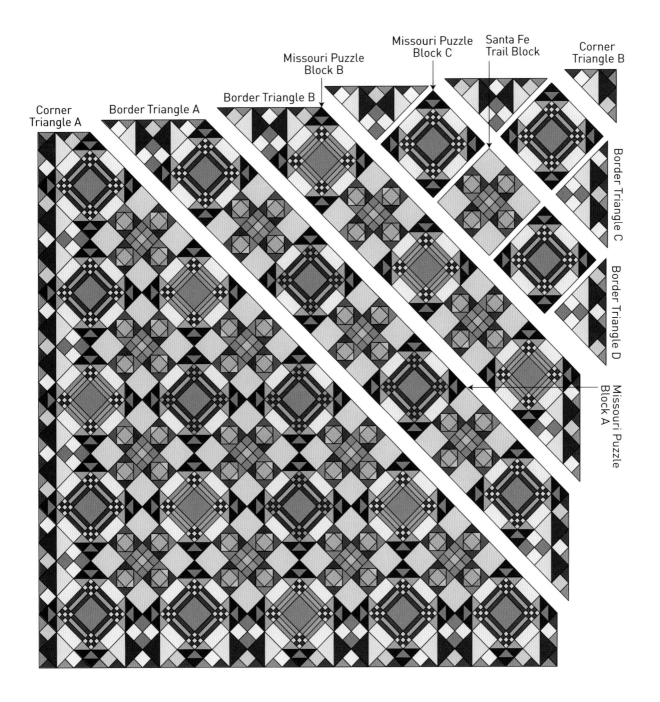

Corner Triangle A

Border Triangle A

Border Triangle B

Missouri Puzzle Block B

Missouri Puzzle Block C

Santa Fe Trail Block

Corner Triangle B

Border Triangle C

Border Triangle D

Missouri Puzzle Block A

Assembly diagram

Finishing

HUGS & KISSES is quilted edge to edge in a soft, flowing swirl pattern using cream thread. Cathy, the quilter, chose the pattern for the quilting, and she chose well. It is a nice balance to the very angular and square look of the blocks. Dark blue binding pulls the color from the center rail fence units to the outer edge. This gives a nice finish to a quilt that doesn't have traditional borders.

Make it your own

Try a pink, black, and gray version, with a bra print taking the spotlight!

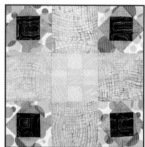

A soft palette with a strong color in the center of the square in a square unit is a delight.

LEFT: HUGS & KISSES, quilting detail, full quilt on page 80.

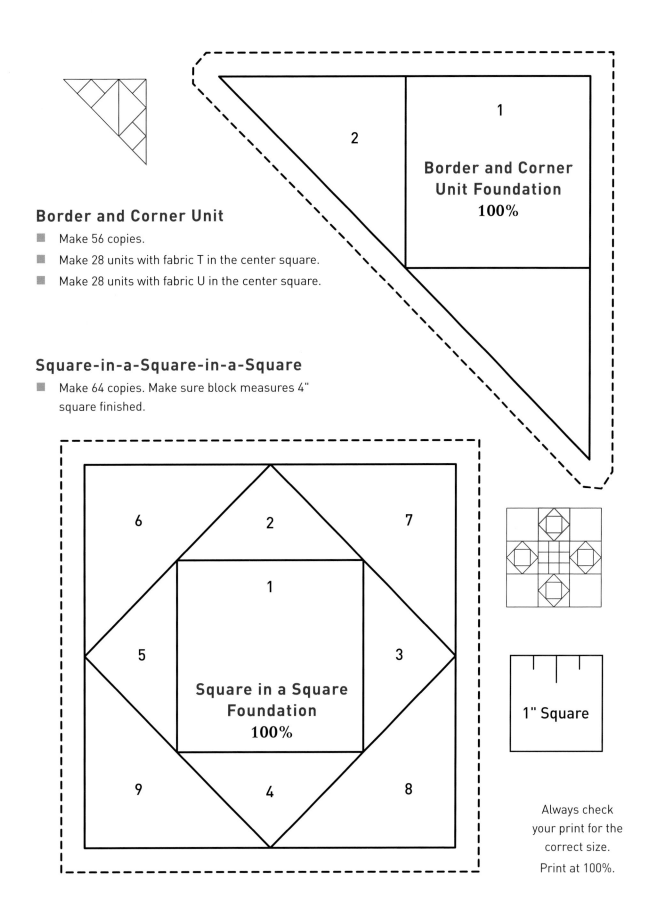

Border and Corner Unit

- Make 56 copies.
- Make 28 units with fabric T in the center square.
- Make 28 units with fabric U in the center square.

**Border and Corner
Unit Foundation
100%**

2

1

Square-in-a-Square-in-a-Square

- Make 64 copies. Make sure block measures 4"
  square finished.

6

2

7

1

5

3

**Square in a Square
Foundation
100%**

9

4

8

1" Square

Always check
your print for the
correct size.
Print at 100%.

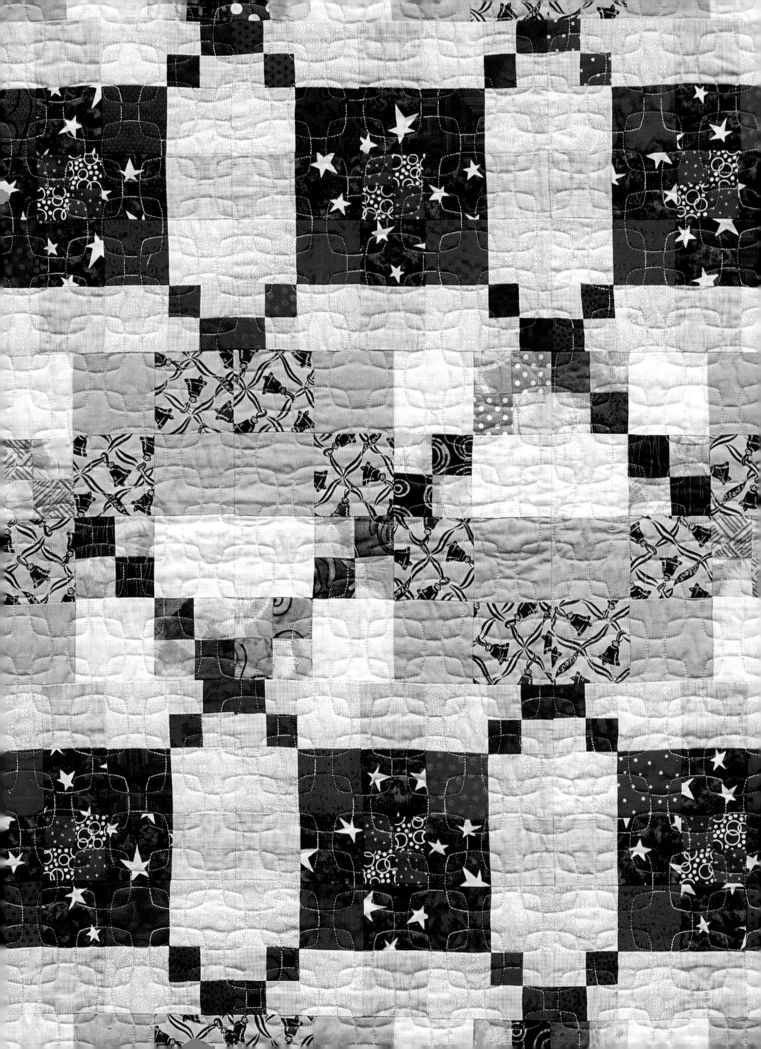

RESOURCE GUIDE

Professional Longarm Quilters

Longarm Bob at Quilters Quest
quiltersquest.com

Arkansas Man Quilter
Eddie Landreth
arkansasmanquilter.blogspot.com

Specialty Rulers

Pineapple Tool
Gyleen X. Fitzgerald
ColourfulStitches.com

Easy Angle™ Ruler
EZ Quilting® by Wrights®
ezquilt.com

OPPOSITE: Woven Argyle, detail, full quilt on page 32.

Wth the publication of *Half-Scrap,* Mickey has truly come full circle in the quilting world.

While known for years as an art quilter, she is secretly a dedicated piecer, at home making bed quilts for her family. If you look closely at her art quilts, you will see traditional piecing found its way into many of them, in the form of backgrounds.

Her books *Pieced Hexies, Ring Around the Hexies,* and *Pieced Hexies Deux* served as door openers to this latest book filled with half-scrappy traditional pieced patterns. After all, it is as Mickey's states: "There is more than enough fabric in the studio to make both art and traditional quilts."

Mickey is happily piecing and appliquéing her days away. She is accompanied by her trusty studio assistant, Molly, her mini doxie. You can join her daily on her Facebook® page MDQuilts, blog, and website mdquilts.com.

OPPOSITE: WABASH5-6830, detail, full quilt on page 52.

#10751

#10753

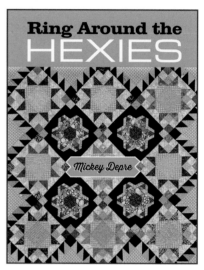

#10755